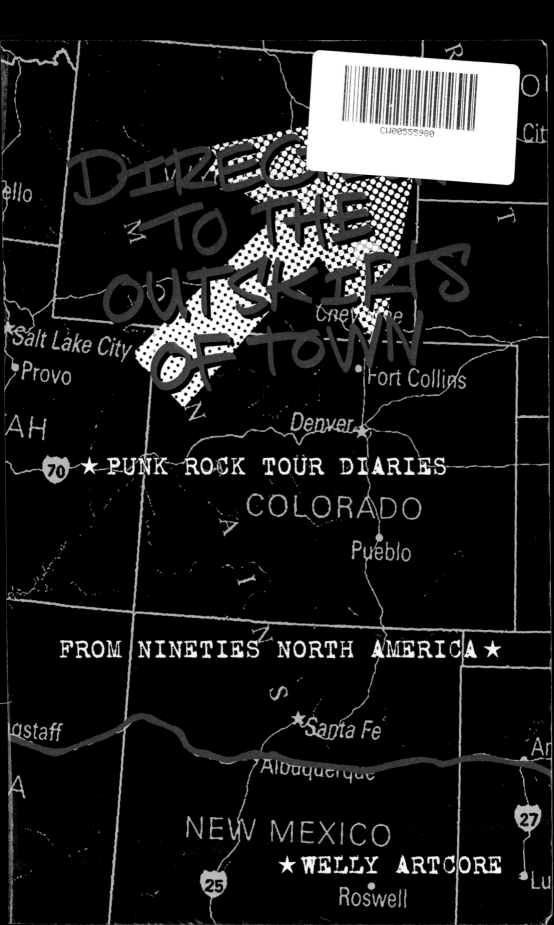

DIRECT TO THE OUTSKIRTS OF TOWN

★ PUNK ROCK TOUR DIARIES

FROM NINETIES NORTH AMERICA ★

★ WELLY ARTCORE

Published by Earth Island Books
Pickforde Lodge
Pickforde Lane
Ticehurst
East Sussex
TN5 7BN
UK

First published by Earth Island Books 2021

ISBN 978-1-8383567-4-3

First edition printed May 2021

Printed and bound by Eazyprint in the UK

www.earthislandbooks.com

DIRECTIONS TO THE OUTSKIRTS OF TOWN

"Stuff your eyes with wonder, he said,
live as if you'd drop dead in ten seconds.
See the world. It's more fantastic than any
dream made or paid for in factories."

Ray Bradbury, Fahrenheit 451

GRINDCORE STENCHFEST!
SUNDAY JULY 10 4PM
CHAOS U.K.
FROM ENGLAND
DISASSOCIATE
AND MAGGOT
PUBLIC NUISANCE
NEW REPUBLIC
TURMOIL
AT
WETLANDS
161 HUDSON ST.
...WHY ARE THERE SO MANY FLIES IN HERE?...

CHAOS U.K
BABY HEAD JULY 12TH
-TURMOIL-
-EDISON-
-LOST CAUSE-

CHAOS U.K
WITH SPECIAL GUESTS
WED. JULY 13TH 1994
AT THE FURNACE TAVERN
155 N. 11th
$5.00

FACTORY
727 W. BROAD · 649-4651
TORNADO PRESENTS: All Ages · 8pm UPSTAIRS
CHAOS U.K.
From England
ONE HUNDRED PERCENT
TWO FINGERS IN THE AIR
PUNK ROCK

ENGLAND'S PUNK LEGENDS
CHAOS U.K.
AND
EYEHATEGOD
Tuesday
10PM July 19 PUNK
$5
14000 n. nebraska tampa 971-0078
all ages?

ALCOHOLIC SLUTS PRESENT...
CHAOS UK
with
EYEHATEGOD
Free FRIDAY JULY 22nd
RC BRIDGE LOUNGE
1201 MAGAZINE
PH. (504) 523-9190

Monday July 25
CHAOS UK
EYEHATEGOD
ETHYL MERMAN
RIOT SQUAD
ALL AGES
ONE HUNDRED PERCENT
TWO FINGERS IN THE AIR
PUNK ROCK
$5
PRESENTED BY
TWISTED KI
GALAXY CLUB Deep Ellum

SHOWCASE THEATRE PRESENTS
ALL AGES
683 S. MAIN ST. CORONA 880-340-0965
NOW OPEN
WEDNESDAY AUG. 3
CHAOS U.K.
DOORS 9P.M.
ONE HUNDRED PERCENT
TWO FINGERS IN THE AIR
PUNK ROCK
PLUS SPECIAL GUESTS
IN THE AIR

FRIDAY AUGUST 5
CHAOS U.K.
EYE HATE GOD
ACME INC.
SLIP
$6
CACTUS CLUB
18 AND OVER WELCOME

RENO 94
CHAOS U.K.
It's A Swindle, Man's!
EYEHATEGOD
Toxic Narcotic
UNISCENE
NoiseGate
GAUGE
MONDAY AUGUST 8TH
$6 · ALL AGES · 7PM
FALLOUT SHELTER / RENO · 702-324-3000 for info
PUNK FEST

CHAOS U.K.
SWINGIN UDDERS
MISERY
ASS RASH
AUGUST 19th 8 PM
ALL AGES FIVE BONES

FROM ENGLAND
CHAOS UK
NEW RED ARCHIVE RECORDS FROM SAN FRANCISO, CA.
THE SWINGIN' UTTERS
AND PUNKS FROM SOUTHERN, CA
THE MAGGOTS
THU. AUG 25
18 & OVER 10 PM
DOORS AT 9 $6
GROG SHOP
1765 COVENTRY CLEVE. HTS
321-5588
THREE CHORDS AND FUCK YOU

DIRECTIONS TO THE OUTSKIRTS OF TOWN

PUNK ROCK TOUR DIARIES FROM
NINETIES NORTH AMERICA

CONTENTS

1994

1998

FOREWORD BY KAOS

In the summer of 1993 I nearly died! Two litres of Absolut
Vodka on an empty stomach, drunk in about thirty minutes
flat showing off in a Minneapolis squat, on top of two
months worth of assorted other poisons, more 'top of the
range' amphetamines than an entire United States bomb wing
(circa 1965), with little to no food and accompanied by
about a hundred CPH (cigarettes per hour), very nearly saw
me off.

As I lay there exhausted, breathless and blue in a foetal
position on the floor of the tour 'bus', I could hear
them banging on the panels and screaming, "Come on Kaos,
fucking wake up! We got a litre bottle of brandy here with
your name on it!"

I remember thinking as I drifted in and out of my near
death experience, "Fuck the U.S.A., never fucking again."

A year later Chaos U.K. were at their peak, with arguably
our greatest line up. We had already spent a decade touring
the entire world non-stop, and woe betide me here we were
off for the second time to the United States, though this
time accompanying us for the entire tour of duty, taking
notes, photographs and the piss, was a young Welsh lad
called Welly, who wrote a fanzine called 'Fartcore!' Or
something.

Now normally I can't remember shit, when it comes to tours,
gigs and the like. Most memories disappear in a hedonistic
haze that would have had GG Allin throwing in the towel
(see 1993), but this time, someone wrote it all down! And
now some fool has offered to publish it, so here I am
writing a short foreword of sorts.

It will come as no surprise to most of you, to learn that
C.U.K spent an inordinately long time in the pub. Whether
we were on tour, recording, rehearsing or performing. We

were fuelled by alcohol, for decades it was the lifeblood that oiled the engine.

And it worked. But by God the USA was sent to try us. 99% of our tours left you with the kind of PTSD you could only pick up in the jungles of Vietnam, but in 1994 and in deepest darkest Bumfuck, Ohio, we took touring to a whole new level of trauma, and we "learnt to love it!"

All our US tours including the one that nearly killed me, were a lot of fun, potentially fatal, but a lot of fun nonetheless, and Young Wellington has stirred a lot of memories with his 'booklet'. Names of bands and people who I had long forgotten, and who I hope are all still in the best of health. The now infamous letters to 'Dear Maximum Rock'n'Roll' which nearly ruined our already ruined reputation. Plus the highs, the lows and the pure insanity of it all.

So without further ado, I bid you all welcome to that long hot summer of 1994, get on board the fucking bus, America here we come!

Kaos, Bristol, U.K. 2021

PROLOGUE: REAR-VIEW MIRROR

When people think of punk rock touring in the Nineties it's often perceived differently to the romanticised view of the Seventies and Eighties and viewed through the lens of the more commercial side of punk that took place. But while all this was going on the DIY level bands continued to tour in exactly the same way as they always had, with tours set up by phone or mail with punk kids putting on gigs and even for a lot of the original hardcore era bands such as CHAOS U.K., YOUTH BRIGADE and 7SECONDS you'll read about herein, nothing had really changed and they carried on regardless as a sort of bridge between the then and now.

The two tours you're about to read happened a generation ago. My son is now the age I was when I hit the road the first time in 1994 and a lot has changed in that time. The advent of mobile phones, the internet and GPS technology have all become ubiquitous to make life more convenient, a luxury not afforded us at that time. Looking back, the absence of this technology probably made it that much more exciting, you couldn't Google ahead to see what anything looked like or what to expect, and contacting anyone meant pay phones at gas stations, truck stops and motels. You were literally blind to what was coming down the road. I'm not saying it was harder, I'm just saying it was different.

As the memories fade and stretch off into the murky past, I'm glad my DIY punk rock journalistic nature saw me take those empty journals with me and scrawl down everything that happened day by day, writing it all out in detail on my return home, my rudimentary photography skills keeping a visual record on my old Pentax P30, and not just of the bands, but of everything along the way. These tour diaries first appeared in a rougher form in the fanzine I make, Artcore directly following the tours, but I've now revisited and rewritten it all here in far more detail. So without further ado, grab your bag and jump in the van. Next stop, nowhere...

1994

CHAPTER 1: THE LONGEST INDEPENDENCE DAY

July 4th 1994 had been a day like any other until my friend Marvin rang the bell of my flat and I bundled my old army rucksack into the boot of his dad's car. Even though I'd seen them play a few times, I barely knew any of this legendary band CHAOS U.K. apart from Marvin, but this changed rapidly over the course of the next few hours. An hour or so later we greeted the rest of his band at Bristol bus station and queued up for a coach to Heathrow. Our luggage stowed, the vocalist Chaos said loudly, "Get on board the fucking bus, America here we come!". We followed him onboard and took our seats.

Chaos was the vocalist, makes sense right? He used to be the bassist and was the only original member. Urban combat pants, boots and band t-shirts, usually copped from a variety of support acts. His head completely shaved and shining, he had an air of authority about him, and had acquired the moniker of The Colonel. With a wry sense of humour and one eyebrow raised, he wouldn't have been out of place in an episode of 'It Ain't Half Hot Mum'.

Guitarist Gabba was the quietest of the lot. Cropped hair, a sly eye and a slouched posture, usually occupying himself by eating, fiddling with things, and making stuff out of whatever was at hand, just like a kid would, along with prodding people and throwing missiles he had constructed. Like a living, breathing cartoon character.

Marvin was the bassist, tall and thin with spiked hair, boots, ripped jeans and a torn denim jacket. He was regularly loud, over confident and often hilarious, like a cross between Sid Vicious and a 70s British TV comic. I'd known him since the late 80s, and knowing him was the reason I was there.

Pat, or The Devilman as he was called, slurred like a drunk and his conversations were brief, obscene and usually culminated in insane cackling. A shaved head and goatee beard he had the strange habit of doing a little Irish jig, especially while clutching a pint glass or two, sloshing foaming ale, or preferably cider, all over himself. He wore beaten up old Converse trainers, loud Bermuda shorts and spoke like a true Bristolian. Back home he worked in a greasy spoon café called Munchers and was a scooter boy who rode Vespas and Lambrettas.

After a lunchtime pint at an airport bar, our British Airways flight to New York took off at 3pm, and after an excruciating wait for the toilet light to come on regretting that pint, the following eight hours were a succession of profane conversations, and extended bouts of hilarity at largely inane things, while consuming tiny cans of lager.

About two thirds of the way through Chaos fell asleep in a drunken stupor and Gabba wrote 'A.I.D.S.' on his neck in permanent marker (real name Adrian). He promptly came up in a rash and was less than amused upon waking to also find a sanitary product forming a makeshift Mohawk on his baseball cap. Marvin disappeared and was later located sat next to a female flight attendant occupying two seats behind a drawn curtain. Gabba threw paper aeroplanes while The Devilman cackled loudly his oft repeated catchphrase, "Ha ha ha, that's outraaageous!". I sat and observed, taking photos of my new found friends, wondering what I'd let myself in for.

Just after 6pm local time, the 747 banked heavily and New York City arched into view, zooming in like a dramatic shot from a blockbuster movie under the burning glow of an early evening sun, casting skyscraper shadows across the River Hudson. We craned our necks from the centre row of seats to catch the view from the windows, before stumbling out into JFK airport and nervously passing through immigration.

Once on the other side The Devilman approached us in his flaming Bermuda shorts and ratty pink Converse trainers laughing, "That guard was a right zoomer, he asked if I was 'ere for the Gay Olympics! That's outraaageous, ha ha ha!" We exited the airport to meet with our local host and the band's guitarist Victor Dominicis, a native New Yorker of Cuban descent, he ushered us into his mother's car for the drive to their apartment in Queens.

Victor had first played guitar in HELLBENT and SACRILEGE, before playing bass in New York legends REAGAN YOUTH in the latter half of the 80s, and then formed NAUSEA before joining CHAOS U.K. Victor was quiet, dressed in black, and was usually unshaven, delivering dry and cynical New Yorker quips out of the side of his mouth. You had to be quick to catch them, and even quicker to catch on.

The next thing I knew I was sat in the middle at the back of this huge old sedan that bounced along on what seemed like huge springs, and the windows were wound down to let in the aromatic city heat. Next to me, Gabba reached into his bag, leaned forward, and pressed a tape into the cassette player, and as we traversed the bridges of New York, the strains of "I'm A Cider Drinker" by the Wurzels blasted out of the speakers at full volume.

Alongside the honking horns and July 4th fireworks, this scrumpy soundtrack added even more to the culture shock as I gazed out of the window and observed the passing city streets under the smoggy sienna haze of a New York summer sunset, and inhaled this strange new humidity and sewer bouquet, all to the sound of the Wurzels.

After half an hour we arrived at Victor's apartment on Ketcham Street in Elmhurst, Queens where we were to spend the next few days while they rehearsed and acclimatised before their impending campaign across this God fearing continent began. It felt like black storm clouds loomed on the horizon, something unseen urging me to go back.

3

CHAPTER 2: WALL STREET CRASH PAD

"Good morning jet lag!" Came the wake-up call from bassist Marvin. After a rough night's intermittent sleep I was beginning to find out what that felt like as the bodies scattered all over Victor's room slowly came to life. "I'll Jet lag you in a minute", came the reply from The Devilman lighting a cigarette, his face barely visible from his sleeping bag.

"Anyone want some cwoffee?" asked Victor, "my mother's out of town for the week so we have the run of the place." "What's that fucking smell Vic?" Came Marvin's unsubtle query. "Fuck off, it's the cat's litter tray in the bathroom, we're on the fifth floor man, all the pets live indoors here." The ammonia aroma quickly seeped into your every pore, there was no respite.

The first thing that hit us when we stepped outside the apartment block escaping the smell of cat urine on Tuesday the 5th of July was the stench of New York refuse. Victor needed to go to the Post Office so we waited on a bus stop somewhere while a nearby clock high on a building notified us that it was 103 degrees Fahrenheit, and I stood there feeling faint surrounded by concrete and steel.

"Have you booked any practice time Vic?", asked Chaos during the short bus ride. "Yeah, three sessions starting tomorrow." We alighted the bus, walked up some grand steps past some columns and into what I thought must've been a museum, but it was just a Post Office that looked like a grand City Hall back home. Pat's voice rang out across the echoing hall "When are we going to Mona's Vic?" "All in good time Devilman, all in good time", came the response.

We headed back to Vic's place and then he drove us out to the Devilman's requested local, Mona's Pub on Avenue B in the East Village, a few blocks from Tompkins Square Park. A British style watering hole that should've had a sign in the window that read 'more punks, more dogs, more Irish', with faux-English 'lager' that had the density of Guinness, the flavour of unemptied ashtrays and a hangover that far outmatched its effects.

Mona's was a long and narrow, dimly lit bustling bar filled with people shouting into each other's ears while others squeezed past, and after hours of drinking we ended up leaving at the closing time of 4:00am, but not before the Devilman accused the bar staff of stealing all his money (in exchange for drinks) and promptly disappeared. Chaos was so drunk that after we drove back to Vic's he grumbled and resisted in the back seat, waking only to aggressively push people away, and had to be left inside a shuttered private car park for the night only to awake to a hangover the size of the Empire State in the searing heat of an underground New York car park in early July.

The band had three rehearsals lined up before the tour at a space that Victor had booked, so we headed there on the subway for the first practice on Wednesday the 6th July, and us confused Limeys had no idea where we were except at one point, as the graffitied subway train rattled from underground to overground passing seemingly endless girders, Victor pointed out that we'd entered the Bronx.

At the practice room some local punks had turned up to watch. It was another baking hot day and I sat against a wall while CHAOS U.K. ran through their set a couple of times, and after a few hours of noise we got a bus back to Queens and Vic's apartment.

On the following day of Thursday the 7th July I skipped the following practice and walked around Elmhurst on my own, taking in my new surroundings and still feeling like an alien in a strange town. I found an art supplies shop on a street corner and decided to buy some acrylic paint and a brush as the artwork on my old leather jacket was worn out and cracking under many layers of paint.

Friday the 8th of July rolled around and while they were at their third practice, I cracked open the acrylic, sat on Vic's bed and selected some record covers from his collection for a new design. I settled on MDC's 'Multi-Death Corporations' tank by Vince Ransid in the centre, and the CRUCIFIX logo at the top. After I'd finished painting, the band returned with the good news that they'd purchased a bass head and cab from the practice room for $250.

Three rehearsals deep and CHAOS U.K. were on form to take the States by storm. The tour organisers though showed some early signs of incompetence when Victor, Marv, Pat and myself took a three hour drive to Cherry Hill in New Jersey on Saturday the 9th July to pick up the lavish rock excess tour coach, and home for seven weeks, and it turned out to be a Dodge seven-seater family buggy with sliding side door for the kids.

Smaller than your average American motorbike, it did have air conditioning and a stereo, so at least it was relatively more comfortable than a cattle truck. "Where are we going to put the fucking drums Vic?", asked the Devilman before his usual cackling commenced, "Ha ha! That's outraaageous!"

The van was brand spanking new and Marvin, Pat and myself entered the vehicle to the aroma of factory-fresh upholstery and carpet. Marvin promptly trod chewing gum into said carpet and instructed me as he pulled away to follow Victor back to New York, "Oi Welly! Take that big sticker off the back window will ya? I can't see out the back".

I set about the task at hand and it was well adhered to the glass and ended up in pieces in the process of me scraping it off with my fingernails. It turned out to be the temporary number plate, and we had to later meticulously piece it back together with tape. Rather than seven weeks sat on top of amps in the family minivan Victor later phoned U-Haul and rented a trailer for the back line.

Meanwhile back at the ranch, Chaos and Gabba had decided to go out, deadlocking the apartment door for which Victor had no key, and was less than amused upon his return. "You can blame him!" proclaimed Chaos, and Gabba returned the accusation, and back and forth it went like an impromptu hallway homage to Laurel and Hardy. A locksmith was called and he sorted it out for $75, not bad for five minutes work.

Then came the discovery of Taco Bell. Being a vegetarian was no joke in the land of Beef Jerky and 'Intestines and Gore' on the menu at the local takeaway, and you couldn't survive on pizza, well you could, it just wasn't advisable. So this cheap veggie Mexican fast food, that filled the gap and tasted alright when covered in eighteen sachets of hot sauce, became the basic tour diet for the next two months.

That evening we all clambered back into Vic's mother's huge sedan and Vic drove us like the Anthill Mob to somewhere in Brooklyn. We pulled up under a street light somewhere outside a house where a group of gentlemen had retired to the stoop to enjoy their after dinner cigars.

"Stay here, I won't be long", ordered Vic and we sat there, all British looking, sheepish and mildly terrified under the buzzing gaze of the street lights, avoiding all eye contact with the exotic cigar smoking gentlemen. Sure enough, five minutes later Vic returned with a wry smile, didn't say anything, and drove us back to Queens.

CHAPTER 3: RISE AND SHINE, UP AND AT 'EM!

The first gig loomed and the unknown wonders of the legendary New York punk scene were swirling in my brain, so on Sunday July the 10th we headed off to a club called 'Wetlands' at 161 Hudson Street, down by the er, Hudson. What did CHAOS U.K. mean to America's downtrodden youth? Was 'Cider I Up Landlord' an anthem for a whole generation or just a soundtrack for mindless violence? I was about to find out.

It was early and nothing was happening at the club so we wandered down Laight Street to the river as the wind whipped down the high rise city streets off the water, even on this the sunniest of days. We followed Battery Park Esplanade a mile or so south until we could see the Statue of Liberty in the distance and stopped to take photos of each other. We then turned around and gazed up at the World Trade Center climbing off into the stratosphere behind us.

The 'Wetlands' was a large dimly lit warehouse with a wall-sized psychedelic mural of a hippie gathering in a park, including a mock tour van festooned with touring bands' stickers. Roy Mayorga, formerly of NAUSEA, was going about his business on the P.A., four free drink tokens were exchanged, and first up of the day, billed as a 'Grindcore Stenchfest', were ASSRASH, Minneapolis drunkards whose reddened faces looked like they'd spent the day engaging in excessive alcohol intake. Their music bore this out.

After ASSRASH had executed their Brit-style brutality on an unsuspecting, almost sober audience, TURMOIL appeared on stage. There had been rumours that these guys were doing the first leg of the tour as they were label mates of the CHAOS U.K. boys, and they were er, straight edge? This could be interesting. They moshed their metallic hardcore to an unimpressed N.Y.C. spiky punk crowd, looking very young with their baggy jeans and baseball caps, and doing the sore thumb routine amongst the growing crust crowd that was starting to resemble a steaming, drunken swamp.

NEW REPUBLIC were a bizarre interlude before DISASSOCIATE (ex-JESUS CHRUST) did their bleurgh-aaargh-woof-woof routine with the imposing Ralphy Boy on microphone abuse, their tiny guitarist sporting a levitating baseball cap. I missed MAGGOT play whilst visiting the local booze outlet to pick up a regrettable 40oz bottle of Olde English 800 Malt Liquor, but caught the end of their slow metallic dirge, before DEFIANCE from Portland jumped up and jumped around to promote their recently released debut 7". A high energy Brit-style attack in an old school anthemic way. Fists in the air, spikes everywhere, and the traditional Portland big bloke on guitar.

Next it was CHAOS U.K.'s turn and the crowd jostled like the huddle at the start of a marathon, some vied for position at the foot of the stage, others squeezed their way into the already sweating fray, while the band wound them up with an intro tape of an old children's TV theme, Chaos pacing up and down the stage provoking them further, mimicking the voice on the tape, "It's time to brush the sleepy dust from your eyes, rise and shine, up and at 'em!"

Then the room exploded, "She was a girl from Birmingham, she just had an abortion", sneered the shaven-headed vocalist in his LURKERS t-shirt as the crowd surged forward. 'Bodies', spit and missiles took flight while steam rose, and the entire club seemed to be jumping up and down from the front right to the darkest recesses at the back, to a cover of the SEX PISTOLS.

Fists and rude gestures were directed at the stage while others climbed on to join in before jumping back off into the heaving mass of humid humanity. Stage right, a long haired guy in a leather jacket clutching his girlfriend was becoming increasingly annoyed because his view of the stage was obscured by a punk leaning against the back of an amp, and he poked and gestured for him to get out of the way. I looked over my shoulder, and moved a little, but not too much. Hey, I was trying to look like I knew the band.

After about two dozen rapid fire punk anthems it was over. Two teaspoonfuls of British accent, four fluid ounces of scrumpy lyrics, eight packets of stolen Wurzels riffs and a pinch of German capital investment, stir violently for thirty minutes, knead for twenty, and leave to cool for two months until the return gig at the end of the tour.

The next day, Monday the 11th July was spent walking around the St. Marks area, looking in record shops, and visiting CBGB's with Val of JESUS CHRUST, before congregating later at Greg from MAGGOT's apartment with Roy from NAUSEA and Jimmy from PUBLIC NUISANCE. We sat around chatting and then followed the locals up the stairs to the roof, where standing atop the apartment building with the lights of the New York skyline spread out before us, the local punks impressed their British punk heroes with an amateur fireworks display. Roy pulled them out of his backpack one after another while Jimmy set about lighting the fuses. Phweee! Pop! We stood there watching them light up the adjacent skyscrapers while the gentle night time breeze brushed the aroma and city heat past our tired nostrils.

"Argh! For fuck's sake! My head! Watch what yer doing ya zoomer!" My Gotham style daydream searching for the Bat Signal was rudely interrupted by the feather light Devilman copping a rocket to the side of his shaven bonce and nearly falling off the edge into the gloom and sirens. After that had put a dampener on proceedings we all headed back downstairs to the apartment laughing at his misfortune.

It was getting late so we bid farewell to our friends, promising to catch up again on our return at the end of the tour, and we returned to Vic's apartment for one last sleep before we hit the road for two months around America the following day. I lay there in the dark listening to the snoring in my brand new sleeping bag from Macy's, and stared at the ceiling with a feeling of both excitement and dread at the coming unknown. Just what was waiting for us in the coming weeks? I was about to find out.

At around 2pm on Tuesday July the 12th 1994, the CHAOS U.K. road machine came to life with a purr and we headed off to downtown Providence, Rhode Island via leafy Connecticut. Independence heartland with matching houses we arrived about three hours later in the late afternoon, and the town with its clock tower seemed deserted as we located 'Club Babyhead' at 73 Richmond Street. A large space, it was dark and windowless with the stage in the far corner and the hours between arrival and opening ticked slowly by with setting up and sound checks. This was where my role in all this became apparent. I was the merch guy and my job was set up the stall, hawk the band's wares, and sort out the cash. Marvin walked up to me in the gloom, "Here ya go, have this." He handed me a key ring with van keys, bottle opener and a variety of tactical implements I would need for the following two months combat in the punk wars. I took them, and it felt like I'd passed an initiation, crossed the Rubicon, beyond the point of no return.

I strutted across the room back to my station at the merch table rattling my new set of keys trying to look like an actual roadie, but failing miserably, and pretty soon LOST CAUSE, EDISON and TURMOIL captivated the audience with their American hardcore sounds. CHAOS U.K. ripped it up yet again to an enthusiastic audience that consisted notably of a one Rob Phelps of WURST. A tanned punk with bleached Liberty spikes, he was also kindly putting us up at his homestead after the gig that night.

Meanwhile the first night of the Welly inc. t-shirt stall and covert flyer stealing operation gleaned a successful haul, and afterwards we headed over to Rob's place and his girlfriend opened a bottle of red wine. The traditional homestead looked like it had been built by one of the original pilgrims and an example of early American architecture. It probably wasn't, but there was definitely a different vibe to Providence than New York.

The next day of Wednesday the 13th of July, we doubled back for seven hours to the streets of Philadelphia and the 'Firenze Tavern' at 135 North 11th Street, and it looked like someone's wardrobe. It was an early gig that had started at 6pm so we'd missed the first band THE VILE HORRENDOUS and the place was already full, so we squeezed in past the bar with guitars and amps aloft as TURMOIL fought bravely with the vocal P.A., before finally admitting defeat.

CHAOS U.K. followed with the same futile attempt at defying the laws of physics from the club's high stage to a packed house, before a line of kids in DEAD KENNEDYS t-shirts bought dozens of CHAOS U.K. shirts for the 1994 summer season, and I spotted a guy selling records out of a box on the bar, so of course I couldn't resist those two dollar 7"s by FEARLESS IRANIANS FROM HELL and THE HUGH BEAUMONT EXPERIENCE. Who else was going to buy them?

7"s in hand I made my way to the door where an argument was under way between the club management and CHAOS U.K. The management didn't want to pay the band and threatened Chaos and Vic when they asked them to abide by the agreement, "Cut me some slack" was the exact request, or demand, depending on which way you look at it. I think they got just some of the money, it wouldn't be the last time.

Hardly knowing us, the TURMOIL Youth Corps were kind enough to invite us back to their house for cookies and milk, and a 'Chaotic Turmoil' interview was executed on my Dictaphone on the porch outside the house before we attempted sleep in conditions not unlike a greenhouse, some opting to simply spread out on the front porch and go to sleep.

TURMOIL were two Jons, a Jeff, a Gary and a young Bob on the drums. They were friendly hardcore kids just starting out and had landed a deal with Century Media, meaning they found themselves all clean-cut 'n' shit playing alongside these cider swilling ne'er do wells from the West Country, England. I bet they couldn't believe their luck.

CHAPTER 5: HOW DEEP THE WATERS

Bodies stirred on the TURMOIL front porch in Philly on Thursday the 14th of July, and a brisk four hour roll down the freeway gave rise to Richmond, Virginia. This was a lot shorter of a saunter than I had envisaged before the stench of civilisation began to dwindle. The club, 'The Factory' at 727 West Broad, looked like a professional booking establishment. We hung around outside and Marvin had his picture taken over the road on North Laurel Street outside the aptly named local greasy spoon café 'Marvin's'.

THE BENT were up first playing a kind of D.K. style rumba in strange suits in this big hall with a big P.A. and twenty or so young members of society. TURMOIL and CHAOS U.K. did their best to entertain the minimum capacity crowd while some guy spent all night playing Thing from the Addams Family, trying to creep his hand into the box next to me to steal a T-shirt, but his evening's attempted thievery proved fruitless. Then a rather large gentleman threw a woman down a flight of stairs, and continued to fight a small doorman who tried to stand in his way. Tensions built.

The bands and violence over, we sauntered downstairs for an evening of Latin music and American beer-coloured fizzy caramel water, while a man serving us at the bar spun us yarns about his original member status of a one popular rock combo known as GWAR. Thinking back, he did look a bit like that Dave Brockie fella, but it's all a blur.

Afterwards we walked miles to a local club, seemingly in the middle of nowhere where the 'Taffy Twirl' showed itself for the first time this tour with the incorrigible Marvin shaking his brittle bones on the dance floor. In the early hours we all headed off to a punk house somewhere leafy, and to top the day off the Right Honourable Victor Dominicis added his first notable deep thought for the day, "You'd better make sure you know how deep the waters are before you jump in the pool." The mini-van fell silent.

CHAPTER 6: A PISS IN THE ATLANTIC

I awoke early as usual on Friday the 15th of July surrounded by boxes of CDs and I presumed that these guys were running some kind of distribution or a record shop, either that or they'd just robbed a warehouse. The house was old and large and I noticed that the garden was overgrown as I stepped outside into the new day.

I decided to take a walk, and the Richmond morning sun shone as I explored the local area alone. It was a warm and pleasant morning and everything you'd imagine Virginia to look like. I'd always been an early riser, accordingly not so good at partying, but it had the advantage of giving me the opportunity to jump in the shower and then explore the locale while the partiers were all still asleep.

When they finally awoke, we headed off to a local punk squat in a warehouse where each person's 'room' was separated by a sheet, before picking up the gear from the 'Factory', who'd kindly let us leave it there so we could go out on the town the night before. Van loaded, we then walked down the street to a local curiosity shop inside a house called 'World Of Mirth', above an alternative store called 'Exile', at 822 West Grace Street. A strange place full of the weird and wondrous oddities of all kinds, you could even buy plastic ants by the ounce. We browsed the bizarre bins and I bought postcards of pinheads, devils and the original photo from Plastic Surgery Disasters to send home.

Years later the entire family of Kathryn Harvey, the woman who created 'World of Mirth', were murdered and their house burnt to the ground on New Year's Day 2006, although the store still exists to this day at a different address. The 'Factory' is now a Wing and Taco restaurant, Marvin's is gone and West Grace Street has been completely redeveloped.

We hit the asphalt towards Norfolk, Virginia, and bored, we started a rude gestures competition with the TURMOIL

14

van who were in convoy with us and had now completely given up any notions of a serious straight edge image. I lost the competition when I threw the V's like Vyvyan from the Young Ones at what I thought was the TURMOIL van but it turned out to be an identical van carrying a group of large men staring back at me. I slunk into my seat, my darting eyes wide open, while the rest of the van roared with laughter.

As we were driving I noticed that the environment and roadside vegetation was changing the further south we headed, and soon enough we arrived at today's destination. The 'N-Sect Club' at 1916 N. Armistead Avenue in Hampton, Virginia, was a big plush rock palace with a balcony, slap-bang in the middle of a spacious parking mall in the middle of what seemed like nowhere, a night club that you could only drive to... strange. Before the gig we all posed for photos under the huge sign directing people to the club that featured the name in a spider's web.

Regardless of its remote location the place soon became packed and the two travelling bands went down well while people sat around on chrome bar stools sipping cocktails, reflected in the many mirrors surrounding them. It was a strange venue for a punk gig that was for sure.

At the end of the night we were invited to an affluent student's beach house near Norfolk for an all-nighter. The frat party was fairly tedious, so a few of us walked down to the Virginia Beach sands at 3am and witnessed the Atlantic from the other side. The waves rolled in from the engulfing darkness as various punks stood around in the sand while the Devilman waded out, hands clasped in front of him, and he looked back at us with a sheepish grin.

The following morning of Saturday July the 16th we stepped over bodies again and started out on the twelve hour drive to Atlanta, Georgia. The Devilman though, soon realised that he'd forgotten his passport in Virginia Beach and we had to drive back to get it before we hit the road again.

As the atmosphere became more humid and the vegetation greener, the freeway slowly turned to A road then B road until finally it petered out to a muddy track through woodland with little white houses dotted along the road. No people, just houses, with plastic animals in the gardens and wooden cut-out black silhouettes of cowboys leaning eerily against walls with bandana neckerchiefs tied on.

Seemingly no people anywhere just twitching curtains, we felt like we were being watched. Finally it dawned on us that we were lost and we decided to turn around in the only available place, someone's front yard. The van typically got stuck on the second point of the three point turn as a pick-up truck appeared and slowed behind us. Vic got the van and trailer out of the rut, and as we slowly drove back the way we came, the truck crawled slowly behind us.

Everyone was feeling a little uneasy at this point so Vic floored it and we got the hell out of there. The truck must've finally decided we were no threat as it eventually turned off, not that we were paranoid or anything. As he got back on the main road it turned out that we were just outside Turbeville, Virginia on Highway 58, right on the State line with North Carolina, and I snapped a photo of a road sign to commemorate the occasion that read "Danville 19 miles, Martinsville 50 miles, Hillsville 188 miles". We had no idea where we were, so we just kept on going.

CHAOS UK

THE REHEARSAL

PAT, WELLY AND VAL (JESUS CHRUST) OUTSIDE SOME CLUB

THE GANZINI BROTHERS (MARV AND PAT) PUT LIBERTY BEHIND THEM

DEFiANCE

NO FUTURE, NO HOPE IN N.Y.C.

disassociate

MURDER THE MIND AT WETLANDS

CHAOSUK

THE DEVIL IN DETAIL, NEW YORK

CHAOS U.K.

WALL STREET CRASH AT WETLANDS

TURMOIL

PROVIDENCE, RHODE ISLAND

CHAOS U.K

PROVIDENCE: 4 MINUTE WARNING

GABBA AT CLUB BABYHEAD

CROWD SHOT PROVIDENCE

CHAOS U.K

NO SECURITY IN PHILADELPHIA

PHILLY CROWD SHOT

CHAOS U.K

DEVILMAN AT THE CLUB FIRENZE

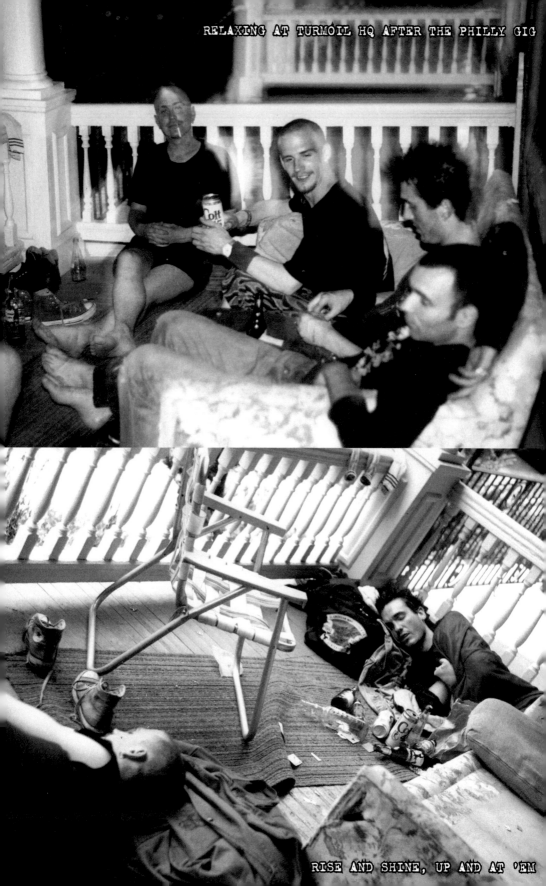

MARVIN'S OPPOSITE THE FACTORY IN RICHMOND

CHAOS U.K

KILL YOUR BABY IN RICHMOND

PLEDGE TO THE EDGE IN VIRGINIA

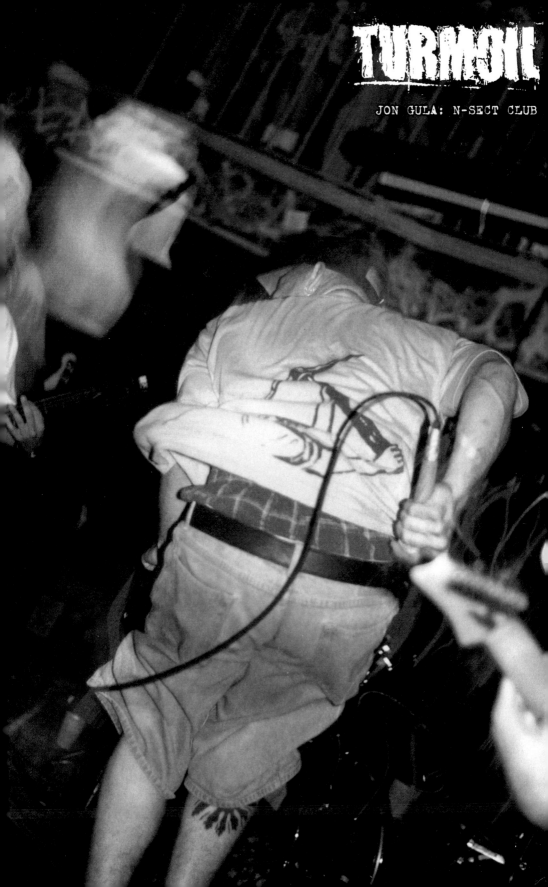

TURMOIL

JON GULA: N-SECT CLUB

CHAOS U.K.

FARMYARD BOOGIE AT THE N-SECT

DEATH FROM ABOVE

VICTOR DOMINICIS AND HIS CHAOTIC ARTERY

CHAOJUK

GABBA AT THE N-SECT

WEST 58 WEST 360

DANVILLE 19
MARTINSVILLE 50
HILLSVILLE 118

ONE WAY

YOU'RE NOT FROM 'ROUND THESE PARTS ARE YOU NOW BOYS?

CHAPTER 7: THE DEVILMAN WENT DOWN TO GEORGIA

After driving south all day through North and South Carolina
we reached Atlanta at about 11pm, but not before getting
lost again on the wrong side of the tracks. When we finally
clunked back over to the right side of the tracks the
Colonel joked, "It's OK, we're safe, look bikers", and
everyone laughed. We discovered on arriving in Atlanta
that we'd been following close behind some heavy rainfall
as there was flooding everywhere. TURMOIL, who had left us
behind by not getting lost had managed to keep up with the
rain most of the way. Gabba interjected with his memorable
quote of the day regarding the long American drives, "Yeah,
but your miles are shorter over here aren't they Vic?"

The 'Sombre Reptile' was a large but dingy club at 842
Marietta Street in Atlanta, policed by some friendly
neighbourhood skinheads who took out their angst on
unsuspecting kids trying to enjoy themselves. Our lateness
saw some of us miss the first band FAILURE FACE loading in,
and TURMOIL had an easy night as the open-minded largely
bald audience left the building for the duration of their
set, before CHAOS U.K., a name taken quite literally here,
served as a soundtrack for more skinhead violence.

Ten plus boneheads beat up one little kid and I had to
hold onto the merch table by the back wall at one point
as a swirling mash of skins moved down the room towards
me. A circle of boots rained down one after the other and
I watched in disbelief as a little punk kid crawled out of
the melee right in front of the merch table, then under the
table to comparative safety on my side.

Thankfully the skins left halfway through the headliner's
set to continue their disagreements in the car park. The
gig over and more t-shirts distributed, tearful goodbyes
were shared with TURMOIL as they were heading home after
their final gig of their week long East Coast leg of the
tour, and we waved them off never to see them again.

After the gig we were offered a place to stay, and as we pulled up outside we realised that it was a skinhead house with a variety of scooters parked outside. We were told they were cool and not in any way dodgy, so we accepted the invitation. These were well-off skinheads who had a big computer set up in their house in a middle class neighbourhood, but we soon discovered that the computer only served as a way to print out sheets of brick wall patterns with the word 'Oi!' on them in 'Oi! The font'.

After a few more light domestic bottles of froth, one of our side-burned skinhead hosts decided to share a little of his political insight with us and stood up proudly to make a speech, "The only reason your country ain't a third world country is cuz you don't have as many minorities". The room fell silent and there was a low murmur as everyone quickly decided to go to sleep, and we got the hell out of there at the crack of dawn while the bald goons lay asleep dreaming of a fantasy Britain that never existed.

THE ORIGINAL COVER ART FOR ARTCORE ISSUE #10

CHAPTER 8: "HI, WE'RE BLACK FLAG!"

Another marathon road stare ensued for six and a half hours to Daytona Beach, Florida, on Sunday the 17th of July, and along the way I recalled the tale to the others of how 80s Florida band STEVIE STILETTO AND THE SWITCHBLADES had written to punk bible Maximum Rock 'n' Roll posing as fans. In the first letter they slagged the band off for destroying a fictitious house they'd stayed at. The next letter praised the band for politeness and doing the dishes.

So it was decided that the infamous CHAOS U.K. would perpetuate the myth of their unruliness and debauchery, and a letter was dictated to me with everyone throwing in ideas, which I hand wrote in my finest scrawl, and we pissed ourselves laughing reading out the finished product as the sun set along the swamplands of Northern Florida.

The letter described the horrible goings by this gang of gobbing punk reprobates later that evening at Ken Barlow's house (a character from British soap opera Coronation Street) at a fictitious residence at 1664 Kronenbourg Drive (a beer) in Daytona Beach, Florida. I posted the letter somewhere along the road soon after and it was published.

Jim Martin of Connecticut and bands MALACHI KRUNCH and BROKEN read the letter, figured out it was a wind-up and decided to write his own letter into MRR with the opposing view, singing the band's praises, saying they'd walked the dogs and mowed the lawn. MRR printed that one as well.

We arrived at 'Black Eyed Susan's', or someone's kitchen unit disguised as a bar, at 530 Seabreeze Boulevard in Daytona Beach, and the British contingent were instantly accosted by some kind of GG Allin fan with an educational problem and a severe lack of self respect. The band soon shook off their new admirer as it was time to meet the next band sharing the roster for the upcoming leg of the bloody trail, a band called EYEHATEGOD.

EYEHATEGOD got on stage to jeers of "hippies" while front man Mike Williams introduced each slow droning sludge metal opus with, "Hi! We're Black Flag", the irony obviously lost on Florida's enlightened mohawk youth. A new band to me, EYEHATEGOD could grind down large Southern slavery monuments with their nihilistic mix of BLACK FLAG and BLACK SABBATH that they emitted at full volume... "Hippies!" Skwee! "Hi! We're Black Flag" Klang! Drone. Repeat. The next leg promised to be interesting.

On first impressions, EYEHATEGOD looked like a bunch of drug addled fugitives who had nothing to live for. There's a lot to be said for first impressions. First there was the vocalist Mike, long hair and a goatee with a sort of distrustful appearance, as if Iggy Pop had grown up in a crack house. Guitarist Jimmy Bower looked like he'd just stepped off the back of a ST. VITUS LP and was soaked in a Southern sauce not to be fucked with. Next up was his guitarist in arms Brian Patton, long straight hair and a goatee hanging from his drawn features. Bassist Marc Schultz was a lanky fair-haired toothless looking guy who openly admitted to actually being a fugitive. And finally Joey LaCaze was on the drums, who seemed to be the odd one out with his smiley face, short hair and friendly demeanour.

CHAOS U.K. did their usual set of rabble rousing punk rock anthems and worked the crowd into a frenzy, and afterwards we hung around in the parking lot skateboarding before we headed the twenty or so feet to the promoter's garage apartment next to the bar's parking lot. The usual tour gibberish and incessant nonsense that was CHAOS U.K. ensued in the apartment, and the madness seemed to freak EYEHATEGOD into disappearing for the night, and in turn the promoter decided he didn't want us to stay in his hovel after all so we got a room at one of the many hotels on Daytona Beach right next to the sea.

CHAPTER 9: LIZARD'S EYELIDS

The road headed to Miami on Monday July the 18th, well, Fort Lauderdale, but we didn't see any signs so we went to Miami first, stopping briefly at Miami Beach with its long stretches of road running parallel to the sea and palm trees. The atmosphere was tropical, and it would rain every fifteen minutes, followed by fifteen minutes of baking heat. Then we drove back 30 miles north to Fort Lauderdale.

The 'Plus Five club' at 5715 University Drive in Davie was a big plush rock club with big bouncers and a big stage that looked like it had been refashioned out of a Target superstore, and I think may actually be one today. Marvin and The Colonel did an awkward interview with Vinny and Sterling of 'Lizard's Eyelids' zine in the searing heat of the parking lot next to the van. A band called CAVITY were first up with their feedback infested GODFLESH style noise. They only had a twenty minute set but were given forty five, so left us with the audio treat of twenty five minutes of feedback with band members rolling around the stage even after the drummer left, leaving Marvin the opportunity to get up for an impromptu drum solo to a confused audience.

EYEHATEGOD got up next and shredded flesh from the bones of the unsuspecting and heavily perspiring Floridian audience, before the CHAOS U.K. crew straddled the stage. Fraught with sound problems Victor promptly went off ranting at the P.A. guy over the microphone, "Hey, it sounds like shit up here, do your fuckin' job!" They actually sounded alright out front, but not on stage, but it did come across as a tantrum to the crowd. Victor was saved from a bouncer assault afterwards by the gibbering of the rest of the band in super fast British lingo.

After the gig EYEHATEGOD disappeared again and we crashed at some mohawk nut's house surrounded by adult mags and rubber gloves. We thought it best to leave swiftly in the morning in case he demonstrated their purpose.

41

CHAPTER 10: AN AMERICAN TRAIL (EVIL GOES WEST)

Before we started the drive to Tampa on Tuesday the 19th of July I was taken to my first American mall. Parked in a vast deserted car park this was the closest feeling to being in the Twilight Zone or Dawn of the Dead I could imagine, and we wandered through the almost deserted mall to canned music doing our finest zombie impersonations.

After the zombie mall experience we headed east across Alligator Alley, also known as the Everglades Parkway, surrounded by endless swampland. Unfortunately we didn't see any alligators but more than our fair share of monsoon storm weather that was a mix of zero visibility, hammering rain and dense muggy air.

We got lost in Tampa on the wrong side of the tracks again for three hours before finally discovering the 'Stone Lounge' at 14609 North Nebraska Avenue, infested with slam hungry punk rockers ready to do their dastardly deeds in the name of anarchy and chaos. We missed SCROG due to our lateness, but this was compensated by vocalist for the legendary PINK LINCOLNS and all-round nice guy Chris Barrows introducing himself after sending me records to review in the past.

EYEHATEGOD were up next to greet a very responsive packed crowd, and as a result their performance was better and for the first time we realised the full awesome mosh power they were capable of. CHAOS U.K. also ripped it up in fine style, building to a crescendo of punk buffoonery and then... krang! Marvin broke a bass string and stood in awe of the technological task before him, mouth and hands agape in a confused manner. Thankfully someone stepped up and fixed it for this true rock professional, and in the intermission the rest of the boys performed 'The Alcoholic' unplugged.

After a lengthy chat I bid farewell to Chris Barrows and he gave me a kiss on the cheek before we were off to our local crash pad for the night and the following day off.

CHAPTER 11: GLEN BENTON AND THE ROOM SIZE REMNANTS

We found ourselves in an apartment on Wednesday July the 20th in the middle of some sort of black mass with the strains of DEICIDE farting from the speakers and GG Allin throwing faeces from the VHS. The high priest was a large Satanic metal guy, all his friends had long hair and we started to think we took a wrong turning at the River Styx. But then someone reminded us it was Tampa, the home of American death metal or something, so we settled down and rested our weary bones for the first time in a fortnight, keeping one watchful eye on our host, the Dark Lord.

The next day, Thursday the 21st of July was spent witnessing overt Satanism via the deathly Devil dude's barbecue and being treated to Voodoo-style New Orleans potato salad courtesy of EYEHATEGOD. We declined the BBQ'd goat opting for the undead slaw, and our bowels were suitably haunted.

Calorifically sated, we headed out to explore this concrete-jungle-within-a-jungle and bought ridiculous amounts of rare vinyl at Tampa's Alternative Record Store at 11502 North Nebraska Avenue, followed by Ace's Records at 1518 E. Fowler Avenue, which was apparently legendary among metalheads.

There were framed photos of a variety of rock legends adorning the tops of the walls running around the circumference of the large store, and I motioned to Marvin and pointed at one, "Ha ha, look there's Glen Benton of DEICIDE", to which Ace behind the counter piped up, "Yeah, Glen's a regular. He's a carpet fitter by day, he fitted all these himself." As his arm guided our eyes downwards to the Evil One's handiwork I made some quip asking Ace whether Glen's other band was called GLEN BENTON AND THE ROOM SIZE REMNANTS, but my colloquial British humour was lost on him, while Marvin thought it was hilarious. Both record stores are now gone, Ace's is a nail salon, fingers not crucifixion.

As we headed out of Ace's into the seemingly endless torrential rain of Tampa, we hopped, skipped and jumped to avoid the huge puddles that spanned the parking lot and climbed in the van. We then popped back to our gracious host's Satanic apartment to say goodbye and grab our bags before heading north to Gainesville via the I-75.

Two hours later, and we pulled into this quiet student town that was missing its students as it was summer. The 'Hardback Café' was a small inviting bar at 232 South E. First Street in a deserted little square. As the hours passed, very little in the way of an audience was making an appearance, so CHAOS U.K. and EYEHATEGOD continually speculated about leaving and blowing the gig off, right up until they went on.

A few people filed in though and local band DON'S EX-GIRLFRIEND played their version of American pop punk, the empty venue not exactly enhancing their performance, before the two touring street gangs of EYEHATEGOD and CHAOS U.K. displayed their talents to an eventually sort of kinetic and enthusiastic small crowd.

During the set I stood next to the P.A. speakers that were on stands by the side of the stage attempting to take photos, but I fumbled and dropped my camera, breaking the flash unit. For the rest of the tour the photos became increasingly art based and blurry as a result. And they were bad enough to begin with.

After the gig EYEHATEGOD decided to drive all the way to their hometown of New Orleans overnight and sleep all the next day before the next gig, and have an easy drive before the next day's set, while we opted to find a cheap freeway motel somewhere in the middle of nowhere and collapsed.

44

CHAPTER 12: TAKE AS NEEDED FOR PAIN

After eight hours of road rumbling on the I-10 on Friday the 22nd of July, passing Tallahassee, Mobile and Biloxi, we arrived in New Orleans, a shanty town in the Deep South draped in Spanish moss, that was apparently a hybrid mix of Southern style hick, French lunacy and Haitian Voodoo. A sticky and delightful sauce for all the family to enjoy.

Eventually, come nightfall, we found the 'Bridge Lounge', next to a bridge, on 1201 Magazine Street near the banks of the Mississippi and were fed with pizza and pasteurised, homogenised and baptised beer. EYEHATEGOD played well but the crowd didn't really care for watching as there were four kegs of free beer as a consumer enticement. CHAOS U.K. then played a sloppy set with a drunken Marvin pogoing with the bass to try and liven up proceedings. It didn't work and everyone settled on a good sulk afterwards.

So after much ado about nothing, everyone tried to forget about it at the all-night bars in the French Quarter, among the cast iron balconies and hanging baskets. Alcohol impounded feelings though and Dr. Jekylls turned into Mr. Hydes until some people we didn't know started brawling in the street, which quickly turned into a 3am free-for-all, and then a gun was produced. At this point even the grumpiest drunks sobered up and we watched from a distance expecting the worst, until two drag queens sauntered nonchalantly right through the middle of the fracas giving the whole thing an air of comedy that soon dispersed the tension.

Afterwards, a well-meaning man bereft of intellect invited us to his house and we enjoyed the comforts of hard wood floor and tropical sweat-sleep yet again. I stared at the ceiling fan and counted sheep, but it was to no avail as my back was stuck to my sleeping bag as the line from that MC5 song that Vic played in the van every day echoed in my head, "The air's so thick it's like drowning in molasses".

CHAPTER 13: DON'T TREAD ON ME

We headed out of New Orleans on Saturday the 23rd of July, passing one of their notable above ground cemeteries on our way out, and continued on the I-10 towards good 'ol Texas on our good 'ol way to good 'ol Houston for five hours, and 'Harvey's Club Deluxe' at 2524 McKinney Street. All encompassing, the Texas heat felt like a wall that made walking quite a feat. The venue was an old building on a corner in what seemed like the middle of nowhere, the gleaming skyline of Houston visible off in the distance as we were as usual, in a run-down industrial area on the edge of town. How we found these places I'll never know.

TREAD were up first and ran through their Texan punk-o-rama to a growing crowd, with their African American vocalist decked out in traditional skinhead clobber warming up the audience with an energetic set. T-shirt sales were up on the CHAOS U.K. stock exchange, while EYEHATEGOD went down like Taco Bell bowel movements.

At one point during the EYEHATEGOD set two overweight bikers bundled in sporting uniforms far too heavy for the temperature, and proceeded to hand out, of all things, KKK leaflets. We turned around just in time to see the vocalist of TREAD who was stood behind us, hand his Harrington jacket to his pal and face the Klan guys, fists raised like an old school street fighter. One biker copped a clout to the jaw before they both ran off into the gentlemens' restrooms, with the skin in hot pursuit. Thankfully that was the last we saw of the Klan bikers.

CHAOS U.K. played somewhat better than the previous nights' inebriated endeavours and locals BRAIN BOMB had been billed to play but had split up. Shawn Bodden from BRAIN BOMB still offered to put us up at his parents' huge house, we accepted and were treated to milk and doughnuts in the morning that were left by his dad on his way to work. Shawn later ended up playing guitar in TOTAL CHAOS.

The Devilman had unknowingly destroyed his deviled shorts through a combination of alcohol piss and sweat rot, so a few minutes silence were given in their honour on the hard shoulder, before we attached a part of one of the legs to the aerial of the van as a makeshift tour pendant. The remains were set on fire on the side of the road, moaning demonic faces belched from the flames, and Marvin consoled the Devilman, beside himself with grief.

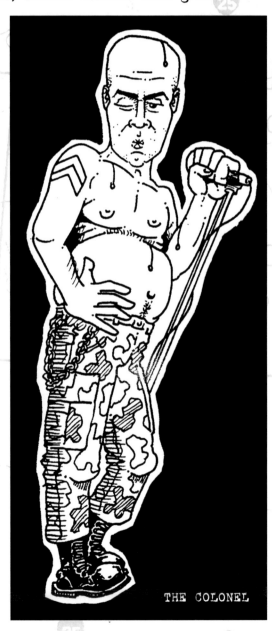

THE COLONEL

CHAPTER 14: OUT TO LIBERTY LUNCH

After a brief shopping trip on Sunday July the 24th for some Dickies shorts to again obscure the Devilman's modesty, we drove to Austin for two and a half hours to the 'Liberty Lunch', a cavernous space at 110 San Antonio Street. The gear was loaded in and an impromptu metal jam consisting of members of EYEHATEGOD and CHAOS U.K. arose from the silence mid-afternoon and became a sort of soundcheck. Two drummers and Vic's wailing Hendrix guitar built to a crescendo but then Gabba plugged in with an intermittent feedback screech, quickly ending the self-indulgent Deadhead jam before anyone could hear it and sign them to SST.

I wandered backstage and there was a 'dressing room', well more like a closet next to the back door, and it was covered in graffiti of some of the bands who'd played there such as D.I. and GREEN DAY. It was still early so we headed across the street and grabbed some food and beer with a game of pool at one of Austin's micro breweries, trying out their 'IPAs' with a little help from the bartender as to what to drink (it'll never catch on). We returned to the venue to hit record level unit shifting on the CHAOS U.K. merch front, while EYEHATEGOD went down like a damp squib.

After EYEHATEGOD had finished I watched from the back of the cavernous hall as CHAOS U.K. ran onstage, guitars aloft, bright lights, big sound, big venue, the crowd surged to the stage and the large club suddenly seemed half empty, but they soon had the place in a frenzy with their expansive repertoire of originals and classic punk covers. While I was manning the merch, a one Rick Magee of local label Turkey Baster Records introduced himself and gave me a copy of his Texas compilation 10" 'Comping An Attitude' for review. After the gig we hit a packed bar and I spotted some dusty but expensive bottles of Dry Blackthorn on the shelf behind the bar, so we skipped the IPAs in favour of the mad apple and talk turned to rural Somerset before we headed off to the land of nod at yet another cheap motel.

CHAPTER 15: I SURVIVED THE CIRCLE

Dallas was the next stop on our strange itinerary on Monday the 25th of July, and we grabbed breakfast halfway in Waco at the historic 'Elite Café' that had a theme all about something called 'the Circle', including books of matches with 'I survived the Circle' on them. At first we thought this might be some cryptic reference to recent cult-like activity in the area, but it wasn't anything to do with the Branch Davidians whose compound was only a ten minute drive away, but a local landmark 'the Circle' next to the café, a traffic circle, or roundabout as they're known in the U.K. Apparently so rare in America, a 'circle' could become a tourist attraction, where people drove from far and wide and competed to see if they could drive around 'the circle' without causing a pile-up, a whoopin' and a hollerin' and shooting their guns into the air in celebration.

After arriving in Dallas and the 'Galaxy Club', a few of the CHAOS U.K. crew headed down to the grassy knoll on Dealey Plaza about a thirty minute walk away and bought photocopied fanzines with photos of Kennedy's brain spilling out onto the mortuary slab. It all seemed a bit ghoulish for a few of us so we looked for record shops instead, failed and found ourselves in a pawn shop, where some broken equipment was replaced, Marvin bought a CD flight case and I found a $1 D.I. tape for the van.

We headed back to the 'Galaxy Club' at 2820 Main Street in the Deep Ellum neighbourhood for a free Mexican food rider. RIOT SQUAD played their Brit punk homage and had some kids dressed up as Dave Vanian and Captain Sensible running around on stage. A little later the Vanian impersonator decided that the best thing to do with his friend's Birthday cake was to slap it in his face. It all seemed funny until it splattered all over the CHAOS U.K. merch table and I was left with the task of cleaning it up, so I collected up the remains, "Hey, call your friend over, the one dressed up as Dave Vanian". Whaaap! He took it in good humour.

After this, a band called ETHYL MERMAN had some line-up issues so they just played 'I Wanna Be Your Dog' for fifteen minutes before the frontman and I traded t-shirts.

EYEHATEGOD locked in and were well received before the CHAOS U.K. legends rocked the house, marred by some salutations from some fans of Adolf Hitler, who were not so well received. After the gig we stayed at this tall skinny friendly guy called Vaughn's house, who replenished Vic's supply of stress relief before we embarked upon what promised to be a hellride through Texas to California.

MARVIN IN A
TAFFY TWIRL

CHAPTER 16: BACK FROM SONORA

The next two days, Tuesday the 26th and Wednesday the 27th of July were spent staring at the road and thinking about the road, followed by some great road watching. We pulled up on the side of the road somewhere in north west Texas only to see a 360 degree panorama of fields and sky, while off on the horizon a rainstorm slowly meandered from east to west, and fences ran by the side of the road for hundreds of miles, hundreds of miles from anywhere.

A rundown motel in Texas with an uninviting pool led to a motel in Albuquerque, New Mexico the following day in the dead of night, until finally on the third day of Thursday the 28th of July, still heading west on Route 66, we just couldn't take any more road. Somewhere in the desert we pulled over for food at a Subway, I was ahead of the others in the queue in my BAD RELIGION T-shirt and after I'd left the woman who'd served me turned to her co-worker in shock and said, "Oh my Lord, did you see that man's T-shirt?"

The Las Vegas gig had been cancelled and all the Arizona dates had been messed with so much Vic wasn't sure what was going on, so it was decided that a bit of tourist action was called for. It must've been the sign back near the State Line of Texas and New Mexico that had read 'Los Angeles 1007 miles' that had done it, so we kept driving west right through New Mexico, stopping at trading posts and roadside attractions along the way, marvelling at native American goods, plastic tourist tat, and drank like vampires from liquor-filled statues of Elvis Presley.

One thousand or so miles later and we stopped at the Grand Canyon for photos, rock hurling and breathtaking views that blew our tiny minds. We looked on as Mike of EYEHATEGOD inched himself out on a precipice just to see what it was like to gaze into the abyss. You'd have thought he'd have done that on a regular basis at band practice to be honest. After a couple of enjoyable hours we hit the road again.

CHAOTJUK

B-B-B-B-BRAIN BOMB HITS GEORGIA

CHAOS U.K

SELFISH FEW: SOMBRE REPTILE

ATLANTA: OUTSKIRTS OF TOWN

HEADING SOUTH MARVIN PAUSED FOR A LIGHT SNACK

SWAMP THING: FLORIDA, WHILE WRITING TO MRR

BETWEEN THE DEVIL...

CHAOS U.K

...AND THE DEEP BLUE 'C'

BLACK EYED SUSAN'S, DAYTONA BEACH

MARVIN INTERVIEWED BY SOME LIZARD'S EYELIDS

THE COLONEL TAKES A NAP IN FLORIDA

EYEHATEGOD

JIMMY BOWER HITTING THE BROWN NOTE IN DAVIE, FLORIDA

EYEHATEGOD

MARC SCHULTZ AT THE HARDBACK CAFE IN GAINESVILLE

CHAOS U.K

LIVE AT THE HARDBACK

NEW ORLEANS: CITY OF THE DEAD

CHAOS U.K

POGO NEW ORLEANS

TREAD

LIVE IN HOUSTON

CHAOS U.K

HARVEY'S: CREAM OF BRISTOL

HOUSTON WITH SHAWN BRAIN BOMB

THE LIBERTY LUNCH IN AUSTIN EMPTY AND FULL

DALLAS: OUTSKIRTS OF TOWN

No essay questions.
5-Minute Loan Applications.

WESTBOUND ON ROUTE 66 AT DUSK

HIGH MILEAGE ROAD SIGN NEAR THE TX/NM STATE LINE ON ROUTE 66

CHAOS U.K

LIVE AT THE GRAND CANYON

WELLY, GABBA AND A BIG HOLE IN THE GROUND

OVER THE EDGE: MIKE WILLIAMS OF EYEHATEGOD

ARIZONA TRUCK STOP: CHAOS, JIMMY, BRIAN, PAT, GABBA, MARV, MIKE

CHAPTER 17: BRIGHT LIGHT CITY

Continuing west through the Arizona Desert tour boredom came to a head while the CHAOS U.K. and EYEHATEGOD vans hurtled down the freeway at full clip, desert on either side, with a cassette fight. As each van took over the other, one would throw an unravelled tape at the opposing van trying to get it to attach, leaving tape streaming off the windscreens and back off into the road. All manner of cheap truck stop cassettes were hurled before a semblance of normality resumed and both vans sped west into the advancing sunset, unfurled tape flapping as we went.

We happened upon the Hoover Dam at about 11pm, it was dark but still about 100 degrees from the hot wind blowing off the desert like a giant hairdryer. As we peered over the edge of the dam we couldn't see much so we hit the tarmac again and gradually, appearing from beyond the horizon came the neon halo of Las Vegas, it's aura emanating from the nothingness beyond the dark chasm of the desert like a beacon for lost intergalactic gamblers.

Before we hit Bright Light City, we pulled over in the desert just to take in the vastness and high visibility of the stars and constellations in the desert night sky. When we arrived in Vegas, as we pulled into a hotel Gabba proclaimed he could no longer talk to people when Vic asked him to go in and book some rooms for the night. Gabba refused, tempers frayed, I stormed in and booked the rooms.

Then it was back to the neon and flashing and the rows of broken people on one-arm bandits trying to reclaim their lost fortunes. This almost happened to a few of our entourage feeding cash into machines before they realised the game was rigged. Free drinks were on offer at the casino if you pretended you were gambling and things quickly got out of hand, and so it became known as the Great EYEHATECHAOSUK Vegas Piss-Up Split EP, and everyone awoke to searing heat and searing hangovers the following morning.

Consuming copious amounts of bottled water while driving
south through the Nevada Desert on Friday July the 29th,
we stopped off at Whiskey Pete's, a Hotel and Casino in
Primm, Nevada, the size of a large mall, to witness the
glass-encased bullet-ridden death car of Bonnie and Clyde,
as well as Al Capone's bulletproof motor, both displayed
within said establishment near the State Line.

Before hitting the road again we paused to take photos for
posterity and then turned south into California through
what we thought at the time was Death Valley, but was
actually Baker to Barstow on the I-15. Then things started
to look a little more Mediterranean with flat-roofed hillside
settlements popping up from time to time, and we headed
onwards and downwards until we joined the Pacific Coast
Highway, taking in the passing beach communities until
finally we arrived at an unsuspecting San Diego.

After getting lost for a good while we found the club the
'Soma' at 3350 Sports Arena Boulevard, and discovered a
large part of this large venue had been closed off, they
obviously weren't expecting a big crowd. We never saw the
front of the club as it was in a little corner mall, and
we pulled up at the back which was just an industrial
area with a fenced-off parking lot. At the back door
the promoter introduced himself and supplied a rider (a
rarity), and then the skinheads came.

The skins skulked around at the rear of the club and one
such lunkhead decided he had known the band personally for
years, introduced himself, and after giving Chaos a bullet
enlightened us to the statistics of his 'Skinhead Army',
"Uh yeah, we got 175 soldiers, 100 in prison, 150 breeders
(his term for women) and 200 kids in training".

Just when we thought things couldn't get any weirder he
went on to describe how he liked to shoot African Americans

for sport and beat up women regularly. This mouth breathing goon who declared his proud ignorance to anyone who would listen quickly found himself talking to an empty room.

The hall of the 'Soma' itself was compact and curtained off and violence erupted regularly in the form of some sort of rugby scrum in the pit. The atmosphere was strange and the place was obviously all run under the watchful eye of the skinheads.

A band called P.O.U.R. were first up and were like SUICIDAL TENDENCIES with GG Allin on vocals. Then the SPENT IDOLS beamed in from 1977 with fluffy coats, make-up, cheap plastic sunglasses, tights, 50s bowling jackets with 'Spent Idols - Punk Rock' embroidered on their backs. It looked like the Californian punk rock circus had well and truly come to town promising side splitting laughs, and they delivered.

The EYEHATEGOD boys entered via the curtains at the back of the stage and went down like a sack of proverbial shit to the boneheads who weren't due to actually experience the gig until a week the following Thursday, so true to form they played ultra slow and FLIPPER-like for what seemed hours, torturing the poor bald imbeciles with their "Hi, we're BLACK FLAG!" drone, pummel, brainwash... "Hi, we're BLACK FLAG!" drone, pummel, brainwash... never mind, forget it, you wouldn't understand anyway.

Of course CHAOS U.K. were much loved by the local primates, but the ring of knuckle-draggers surrounding the front of the stage wouldn't let anyone else dance. The night concluded with Victor getting a punch from one of the follically bereft, and as we were leaving we witnessed one of the master race pistol whip a young kid across a parking lot from the other side of the fence. Thankfully we'd met a guy called Jeff who said he could put us up, so we drove out of San Diego quick smart, past Cardiff By The Sea to sunny San Clemente, where some partied on and some didn't, nervously laughing at what we'd just witnessed.

CHAPTER 19: BEACH BLANKET BONEYARDS

So here we were on Saturday the 30th of July in the sun on San Clemente State Beach looking at the Pacific for the first time, goofing off and being general dorks. The sun, sea and sand all got a bit much for us pastey Limeys after a while though, so we headed to a bar around noon and drank cocktails called Boneyards on San Clemente Pier whilst daydreaming at the sun glimmering off the sea and reflecting quietly about those we'd left at home.

Evening arrived and some bands were playing at a local bar, the 'Doheny Saloon' at 34125 Doheny Park Road in Capistrano Beach, so we headed there for a few homogenised, pasteurised and baptised pitchers of domestic American froth. THE SMUT PEDDLERS were up first, playing tight ANGRY SAMOANS-style punk snot with a Jerry A. type vocalist. These were quickly followed by CHAPTER ZERO who wore baggies and loose shirts and played in a JAWBREAKER vein, all sloppy 'n' poppy.

By this point spirits were running high and the CHAOS U.K. boys were cajoled into doing a few songs after the gig was over. Vic couldn't see the point so he slept in the van while the other four grabbed their guitars and sticks and ripped it up in fine style, and four songs were fallen through backwards before the landlady pulled the plug.

Near the end of the night I got talking to a couple of guys at the bar sporting CHAOS U.K. shirts, claiming they'd bought them off us in Florida and joked that they had followed us to California. They were really friendly and scared us a bit with their fanatical dedication to all things CHAOS U.K. Was this a bizarre coincidence or were we indeed being followed? Paranoia Über Alles.

CHAOS U.K. later recorded a touching tribute to their time in these parts with the song 'Take Me Back To San Clemente' in April 1996 that appeared on the aptly titled album 'The Morning After The Night Before'.

CHAPTER 20: SKATE FOR THE DEVILMAN

Sunday July the 31st was to prove to be a day to remember. The first half was spent at the beach again, our white British bodies sizzling like rashers on the Californian sand as we belly-flopped on belly boards in the shallow end, with our arm floats on like big kids. The night before we'd all been invited to a house party in San Clemente later that day by Josh of CHAPTER ZERO, there was free beer and apparently a double wide skate ramp in the back garden. So of course, the challenge was accepted.

The house party was packed, beer flowed, dozens of skaters skated, and sun-baked West Coast punk blared from the speakers. Then, as was becoming the norm, the CHAOS U.K. boys were gently coerced into playing, so the gear was fetched and West Country cider-punk became the unlikely soundtrack to a small Southern Californian riot. CHAOS U.S.A. hammered out five songs and the ramp started to look like the shred freeway, but then it suddenly all got too much for sun-baked Californian youth and the garden turned into a running brawl that quickly swept through the house and into the adjoining gardens, sending a trampoline flying.

The band played on while Gabba hid behind his amp and I squeezed through the packed party and through the house, headed upstairs and positioned myself on the roof next to a few locals with video cameras who were filming the action, to take some photos of the melee. The fracas quickly ended when the well-off locals shouted "Ghetto Birds!" as a warning and cops turned up in helicopters and cruisers.

The police told us Limeys to leave, but the Colonel was having none of it, flipping them off, "Hey man, fuck the cops!" Actually I made that up, the gear was hurriedly packed and we buggered off sharpish to Kelly the surfer's house to conclude the day's drinking. It was quite something to witness fried American youth get drunk on piss-weak beer and lose their minds to Avon and Somerset hardcore.

It was at this point in the tour that someone switched the Colonel's accent chip to 'California' and he slipped into the local vernacular, "Hey, gnarly rad bitchin' dude, pop a grind, chill out and quit dissin' me, locals only mofo, go figure!" And he was mocked relentlessly for it.

We came around slowly the next day on Monday the 1st of August and took the Wacky Races Freeway north to Los Angeles, Santa Monica, and the Century Media headquarters, to meet the mild mannered Oliver Withöft and his host of German illegal aliens working for his vast metallic empire.

The office turned out to be quite a goldmine of vinyl, CDs and t-shirts, so Oliver promptly ushered us out, checking our pockets as we left, and took us to a local Mexican restaurant where he bought us burritos as we sat along a bar and talked punk rock and the tour so far.

Later back at Oliver's apartment in nearby Venice the Colonel went into cocktail waitress mode, and got everyone steaming drunk on wild concoctions of whatever booze he could lay his hands on from poor old Oliver's liquor cabinet, "This one is called the Ganzini, it's a gurt pokey little number". Oliver just shook his head.

Meanwhile that evening, EYEHATEGOD were recording a radio session for KXLU, and we listened on the radio to the dozen songs and then an interview where they talked about the tour and joked about CHAOS U.K., saying Dallas had been their best gig, followed by Tampa. The next day I complimented them on the set and Mike smiled and handed me their only cassette copy. A few years later Marvin told me that the band didn't even have a copy of it themselves so I copied it for him and he mailed the tape to Mike. Four of these dubbed songs may well have been what ended up on the EYEHATEGOD compilation '10 Years Of Abuse (And Still Broke)' CD with the wrong recording date seven years later.

CHAPTER 21: HANG TEN IN EAST L.A.

We arose early and were down at the Century Media bunker by 9am on Tuesday August the 2nd where an argument was taking place between EYEHATEGOD and the label honchos. CHAOS U.K. joined in after being told that they'd only sold 300 CDs in the U.S. and were confused as to how all the crowds seemed to know all the words to the new songs every night. After the row everyone said goodbye to Oliver and left Century Media for the next gig. We never saw Oliver again and he sadly passed away twenty years later in 2014 aged only 49.

We headed down to Hollywood Boulevard and met up with the EYEHATEGOD boys at Green Hell Records where I found the 'We're Da Machine' 12" by THE EFFIGIES and the first MAD PARADE 12" while chatting with Thrashead of Flipside fame who worked there. We then headed down Olympic Boulevard to East L.A. and the relocated gig at 'Chapalitas' in Boyle Heights (it had originally been booked at the re-opened legendary L.A. venue the 'Hong Kong Café').

The small hall quickly filled with various Latin youth and Y.A.P.O. played a boisterous killer set before EYEHATEGOD blew the power continuously, and then someone apparently broke their leg falling off a wall drunk in the parking lot at the rear. Someone called an ambulance but instead the LAPD turned up - in force - with paddy wagons, sticks and gas, someone threw a bottle and the cops emptied the place. EYEHATEGOD's set was suddenly cut short, CHAOS U.K. didn't even get to plug in, the poor promoter kid was bundled into a police van, and as a result no-one got paid.

While all this was going on I was at the back of the venue by the fire door and I quickly exited through it into the parking lot to find the mainly Hispanic kids all milling around wiping their eyes. Back in the van CHAOS U.K. put the lack of gig and money down to experience and we headed off to Cesar from DOGMA MUNDISTA and SOLUCION MORTAL's tiny hole in the wall apartment in downtown L.A. and slept.

CHAPTER 22: SHOWCASE SHOWDOWN

The morning of Wednesday 3rd August came around fast and we made up for extreme malnutrition at a local café before heading to Melrose Avenue for more vinyl, and I made out like a bandit at stores like Second Time Around where you could find multiple copies of classic L.A. punk albums for $5 a piece. Then we headed out to Corona in Riverside County to a place that looked like a cinema called the 'Showcase Theatre' at 683 South Main Street for a matinee gig. We were treated well and fed well before the bands played; a young band NUMSKULL were first, then VIOLENT OUTRAGE with a Darby Crash impersonator on vocals, DAS KLOWN followed up with an average set, their vocalist's clown make-up not saving proceedings, and then SNAP-HER who were a lively young all-girl old school punk rock band, and the best of the bunch.

I sold a pile of t-shirts and CHAOS U.K. might as well have been THE CLASH back from the dead judging by the rabid reaction when they took to the stage. A ram-raid of a set later and everyone got paid and was happy, as this was a decent club with a friendly owner by the name of Ezzat Soliman who gave all the bands free pizza while TOTAL CHAOS hung around upstairs in the dressing room that overlooked the club looking to pick up hair spiking tips.

After the gig we drove half an hour north to a farm in Fontana owned by a couple, Marci and Gus and their little boy, and drank bottles of beer on their trashed skate ramp with Cesar, James, and these crazy Mexican mohawk slammer kids who were following CHAOS U.K. around Southern California and were always spotted going nuts in the pit.

I recognised Troll, the craziest slammer kid, later when I saw Decline of Western Civilization III with his three mohawks and Abrasive Wheels t-shirt, and the film was a good reminder of the kids we met in Los Angeles at the time. Another kid in the film was wearing the Chaos U.K. shirt I'd sold on the tour, so I guess we met at the merch table.

75

CHAPTER 23: GOLDEN SAILS OF HITS

On Thursday August the 4th we trundled through extreme heat for an hour to Long Beach and the 'Golden Sails Hotel' at 6285 Pacific Coast Highway. Standing around outside we were trying to figure out how a punk gig was supposed to be at a yuppie bar in a yuppie hotel alongside a yuppie yacht harbour, when some posh British woman heard my accent from the other side of the fence, next to her posh boat harboured in the posh marina. She asked me where I was from and when I told her she told me that her parents were also from Cardiff, and I scratched my head. I then spoke to Katz of Flipside outside before the gig, over the hum of the nearby freeway, and then the bands got free drinks and food again.

A variety of misled mohawked misfits trickled slowly into the hotel, as well as the majority of the punks who'd frequented the previous Southern California gigs. First up was a '77-style band whose name slips my mind, then U.S. BOMBS, who I was told featured Kerry Martinez of SHATTERED FAITH and skater Duane Peters of POLITICAL CRAP. New to me at the time, I went up front to check them out, and THE STITCHES were up next with some more old school shuffle.

Soon enough CHAOS U.K. hit the stage and as usual about twenty five people joined them for fists in the air and swinging off the light cage. Nervous, the P.A. guys kept turning their rig on and off so the crowd sang their guts out for a few songs MINOR THREAT-style with no P.A. There was a definite feeling of 'this is a one-off venue' in the air, the light cage didn't survive the ordeal, and then surprise, surprise, the L.A.P.D. turned up with their sticks and tear gas and proceeded to clear the place.

So here I was at the back of this formerly swanky hotel function room behind the merch table, still trying to sell t-shirts as fast as I could when a Robocop approached ahead of the cloud of tear gas, "Exit the building". "Give me a minute, I have to pack up". "Exit the building". "Hang on

76

mate". "Exit the building". So I rammed everything into the big cardboard t-shirt box as fast as I could and exited the bloody building rather than get arrested. Yet another gig shut down. At this point it was starting to feel like C.H.A.O.S. U.K. could've been spelled B.L.A.C.K. F.L.A.G.

Packing the trailer had by now become a fine art and was completed in record breaking time with riot police as an incentive, and then we headed to U.K. Alex's house for an all-night party. Alex was from the U.K. but living in California, and had based his image on Jack from Suburbia, with a bleached flat top and leather jacket with the DISSENSION logo across the back. Alex drove The Colonel, The Devilman and I to a dodgy neighbourhood 7-11 for beer in his beat up Sedan, we grabbed a box of Burgie beer while he addressed the oblivious owner behind the counter, "Let me have one of those Slushies over there, and make it a blue one". Then we somehow got lost before eventually finding our way back to the T.R. House, and SNAP-HER were there partying in the middle of this suburban utopia. They didn't realise they'd be the slums of the future.

CHAPTER 24: SCROTES FROM THE UNDERGROUND

We bailed early on Friday August the 5th, bidding farewell to Alex and the SNAP-HER girls, and the following six hour road haul proved that we knew the way to San Jose. The 'Cactus Club' was a mellow rock club at 417 South First Street where we were handed two beer tokens before SLIP played an energetic set, and then ACME INC. did much the same, their vocalist so desperate for a CHAOS U.K. t-shirt that he traded me his 'Tank Girl' ACME INC. shirt right off his back. EYEHATEGOD reappeared in a puff of smoke after a few days off in L.A. as their band name and God fearing venues had meant they'd had no gigs.

A guy stood next to the merch table then handed us his own hand-crafted full colour version of the gig flyer and was obviously a CHAOS U.K. superfan. EYEHATEGOD brought the house down in grinding style before CHAOS U.K. knocked out their originals and a few covers to a slightly mellower than late crowd. Then the singer of ACME INC. kindly put us up for the night where we found we'd been joined by a guy Marvin dubbed 'Ed the Duck' who invited himself along for the remainder of the tour. Not long after we dropped him off somewhere on a remote highway.

Great itinerary planning part two: on the following day of Saturday August the 6th we had to drive back south to Santa Barbara for that evening's gig at a dark rock venue called the 'Underground' at 110 Santa Barbara Street, not far from the Stearns Wharf pier. This was EYEHATEGOD's last night so we went to Longboard's Grill on the wharf and drank Newcastle Brown on the deck with them and admired the sunset, while managing to clear the place of well-to-do types within minutes due to our punk attire and tour aroma.

Back at the venue, NEUROSIS had arrived in their sixteen wheeled tour mansion three days earlier to set up their sound system the size of a small country in Europe. We missed the SWINGIN' UTTERS debut appearance supporting on the next leg of the tour, then a NAPALM DEATH-style band played, a punk band played, EYEHATEGOD played an intense set in spite of a surprisingly quiet and continually degenerating sound, and the same strangely happened to CHAOS U.K. A ghost in the machine? All the bands sounded appalling.

With my back to the setting sun and the beach, I sat at one of the merch tables that ran along the windows down the side of the club and laughed at EYEHATEGOD as they teetered on their bar stools opposite while downing round after round of Jagermeisters. There was a promotion on for the Devil's cough medicine which was being enthusiastically served to them by smiling women dressed like they were in a German beer hall, and the band gestured for more, glasses aloft like Vikings who'd ventured too far south into Europe.

The NEUROSIS stall was next to me, and I could be wrong but during EYEHATEGOD's technically troubled set they seemed to be taking the piss out of them, "Oooh! Sooo dark! Sooo evil!" EYEHATEGOD's set over, they left for the stage and clouds soon rolled over the barren landscape, Celtic banners appeared on the horizon, the fog of ancient war slowly cleared, the band appeared, eyes rolling back in their heads in the throes of possession from an epoch before recorded history. Behold NEUROSIS, and surprise, surprise, they were twice as loud as any other band that evening. Bzzz! Clunk! As if by some cosmic poetic justice the P.A. cut out, and the audience had to endure three storm-off-stage tantrums before the glitch was finally rectified.

After the gig we all got fed by the venue and headed off disillusioned with the headliners. I'd asked them for an interview, but opted instead to shout abuse at them as we drove off. To top it all off we ended up in a trailer park in Ventura, again half an hour in the wrong direction. We slept rough and felt rough and Genevieve the PR person from Century Media turned up in the morning, turned to me and asked, "What do you think of the Chaos U.K. t-shirt I designed?" "Er, I designed it?!" Of all the people to ask.

CHAPTER 25: BAY AREA THRASHED

We sat around a picnic bench in the early morning of Sunday the 7th of August shooting the breeze under the marine layer of early morning Californian cloud, and no-one was in any hurry to leave as EYEHATEGOD had come to the end of their leg of the tour. Reluctantly, we bid them farewell and they headed off home teary-eyed, except for vocalist Mike Williams who joined us for an all-day drive to Berkeley and 924 Gilman Street.

Hours later we rolled into Berkeley late and missed A.F.I. and the SWINGIN' UTTERS (again). The streets around 'Gilman' were full of groups of punks milling around and some of us hit a local liquor store across the street. Back at the venue it was completely packed so in order to see from the merch table at the back I stood on the table to take in the MDC boys rip it up at the legendary Gilman Street. Almost immediately out of the side of my eye I could see an arm waving furiously. I looked to my right to see some bleach-haired punk kid glaring at me and gesturing to get down as I was shaking the merch table and therefore inhibiting his ability to draw his picture. Draw a picture? This was a gig not fucking art class. I guess he felt a sketch coming on. Thinking about it, that kid looked a bit like that Davey Havok fella. Maybe he was practising drawing Devilocks.

MDC were surprisingly reserved towards the CHAOS U.K. lot and I recalled how back in Texas, Chaos had phoned Dave Dictor and had been told that originally Dave was supposed to be booking the whole tour but someone called Genevieve from the label had phoned Dave and said that CHAOS U.K. were far too big to be dealing with MDC now, and they now wanted so many thousand dollars a gig. Not surprisingly Dave had backed off and was a little pissed off about his wasted time and money, the tour finally being booked by someone going by the name of Mike Kelly. Chaos thought he had sorted it all out during that call, but it did look a bit like Dave had bought the Genevieve line.

Next up CHAOS U.K. did their usual grand performance to an on-stage crowd of revellers and the t-shirts finally sold out as well as my financial backing, as they'd been kindly giving me $1 a shirt to live on. Beano of Bugs 'n' Drugs zine turned up with his girlfriend Jo and ex-Bristol boy Knowsley and we headed off to someone called Gabby's house for a party in downtown San Francisco, where their old friend Sothira from CRUCIFIX turned up for a while for a chat. He was surprisingly small and quiet and I kept expecting him to burst loudly into, "From dehumanization to arms production... it's your choice... peace or annihilation" at any moment. After the party had emptied out, we slept among bizarre sex implements and pro-gun propaganda magazines and tried to figure out if there was a connection.

VICTOR

SUNSET STORM IN NORTHERN ARIZONA AFTER THE TAPE FIGHT

FLIPPIN' OFF VEGAS: JIMMY, MIKE, MARVIN AND JOEY

JOEY, WELLY AND MIKE ACTING METAL

CHAOS U.K. MEETS BONNIE AND CLYDE

WHISKEY PETE'S

FREE MONORAIL RIDES
PRIME RIB DINNER $3.50
MON THRU FRI 3PM TO 11PM
BONNIE & CLYDE DEATH CAR
DUTCH SCHULTZ - AL CAPONE CAR

FLIPPIN' OFF PRIMM, NEVADA

CHAOS U.K

SOMA HOLIDAY IN SAN DIEGO

SAN CLEMENTE HOUSE PARTY PACKED TO THE RAFTERS

CHAOS U.K

THE SAN CLEMENTE BACKYARD TAPES

HOPE YOU GET A FUCKIN' HEADACHE!

WHITE RIOT

THE CORONA LINE-UP

SHOWCASE THEATRE

WED AUG 3
CHAOS U.K.
DAS CLOWN
SNAP HER
VIOELNT OUTRAGE
THUR AUG 4   CLUB EXTREMES
                                    ALL AGES

CHAOS U.K

SHORT, SHARP SHOCK: CORONA

CHAOS U.K.

THE DEVILMAN HITS HIS STRIDE IN CORONA

MORNING BEERS AT GUS AND MARCI'S (CENTRE) FARM IN FONTANA

MIKE WILLIAMS

BRIAN PATTON

EYEHATEGOD

AT THE UNDERGROUND, SANTA BARBARA

MARC SCHULTZ

JOE LACAZE

EYEHATEGOD

JIMMY BOWER AT THE UNDERGROUND IN SANTA BARBARA

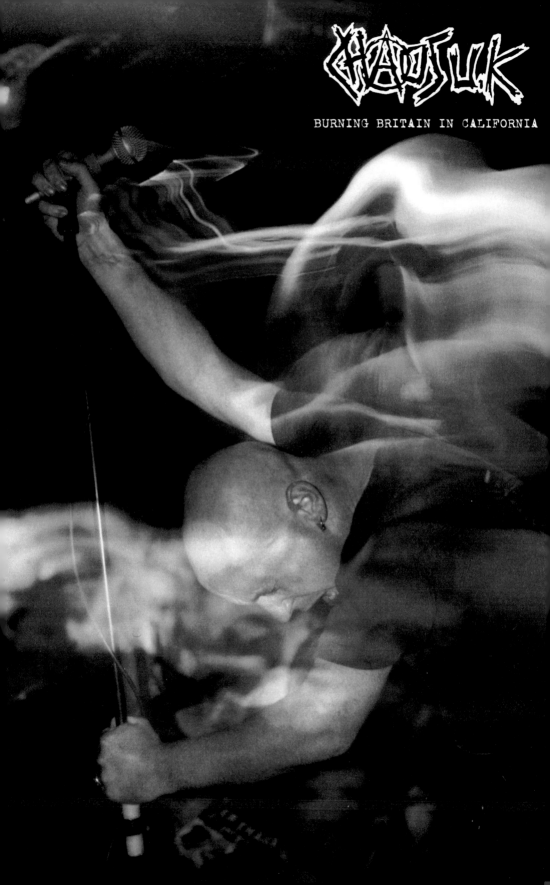

CHAOS U.K

BURNING BRITAIN IN CALIFORNIA

CHAOS UK

HEAD ON A POLE AT THE UNDERGROUND

neurosis

TECHNICAL DIFFICULTIES IN SANTA BARBARA

MDC
AT GILMAN STREET

CHAOS U.K
LIVE IN BERKELEY

CHAPTER 26: THE FALLOUT SHELTER

On Monday August the 8th we grabbed breakfast at a veggie
café followed by a vinyl spree at the 'Epicenter Zone' where
I found 'Creatures For a While' by PERSONALITY CRISIS. The
next thing we knew we were heading over the bridge, out of
California and off to Nevada and the 'Fallout Shelter' at
100 Sierra Street, Reno, with Beano and crew in hot pursuit.

It was Chaos' 21st birthday again so this was an excuse to
try to get drunk for a change on American fizzy beer water.
Challenge accepted, the bands for the night were GAUGE,
NOISE GATE, UN4SCENE, and TOXIC NARCOTIC made their first
appearance and asked if they could tag along for the rest
of the tour, to which no one had any opposition. CHAOS U.K.
played well considering the state of knackeredness they
were in, still not drunk on American beer.

After the gig we stayed at a punk house a mile away across
the Truckee River at 516 Ryland Street where members of
ZOINKS! lived. There were a few fanzine punks in attendance
so everyone was interviewed in a state of sarcasm and
tiredness. Bix Bigler, the original drummer of 'Skins,
Brains & Guts' era 7SECONDS was there, as well as Arjen,
a Dutch travelling Benny Hill lookalike who Marvin and I
hadn't seen since the Cardiff punks picnic circa 1989. He
looked like he'd been lost in the desert for the last five
years, which probably wasn't that far from the truth.

The basement of the house on Ryland Street, which usually
had gigs, was commandeered for sleeping purposes and the
mantelpiece in the living room sported a free zine selection
which helped immensely during Tuesday the 9th of August's
ten hour drive to Eugene, Oregon. Leaving early, it wasn't
until seven or so hours later that we arrived at the 'W.O.W.
Hall' at 291 West Eighth Avenue extremely late, missing
THE RICKETS, TOXIC NARCOTIC, and yet again THE SWINGIN'
UTTERS. This town seemed full of drunks and police, which
promised to be a recipe for something interesting.

CHAOS U.K. played loud and tight to a loud and tight crowd
in a big hall with a big stage and a big sound, and we
spotted our first one-eyed skinhead. Then we headed off on
a wild goose chase to Bruce from the DETONATORS' bar but he
decided against a lock-in with a handful of British drunks
by the time we arrived, so we drove two hours to Ty from
RESIST's house in Portland and slept, except for Marvin
and the Devilman, who talked really fast all night long and
complained that they couldn't eat.

The next day, Wednesday August the 10th, we went absolutely
bonkers in Portland's Second Avenue Records, renowned to
be one of the best in America, so good in fact, that this
proved to be my last big vinyl outing, having to put some
of my armful of albums back in the racks and make do. As we
looked at our records Vic drove the three hours to Seattle
and the Off Ramp at 109 Eastlake Avenue E where I ate my
first veggie burger for over a month. We then visited a
local bar and met Knowlsey's mates from Vancouver, Nick and
others from SUBVERSE, and returning to the gig we realised
we'd missed NOT MY SON and TOXIC NARCOTIC, but finally saw
the SWINGIN' UTTERS, and regretted our earlier mistakes.

CHAOS U.K. played their first really crappy set due to a bad P.A.
and too much beer, it's saving grace being Gabba had been off
hobnobbing with the stars at one of Courtney Love's parties with
Thee Slayer Hippy in the early evening and brought him back
to the gig to sing backing vocals on 'Cider I Up Landlord'.

An actual clown turned up to the gig, some kid who must've
been going to clown school but had forgotten to remove his
make-up before the gig. Either that or it was The Joker,
or somebody put something in my drink, all bets were off at
this point. Bands over, we said goodbye to Beano, Knowlsey,
Jo and crew and they headed back to Vancouver.

After the gig all the bands went to a punk crash pad and it
was a no beer, no smoking, no swearing, 'shoes off please
you might stain the carpet' "party" with some kiddie punks,

so The Ganzini Brothers (Marvin and Pat) performed their drunken jig, "Hey now kid, what's got into ya? What's got into ya kid?" And everyone went to sleep on various floors.

On the following day of Thursday the 11th of August we all sat around and a half-drunk Johnny Peebucks (he got that name from pissing on his money) fell out of a broken window upstairs onto a flat roof, cutting his head on the way. After this we all drove back to Portland and went all Brits on the piss with the DEFIANCE boys with our painted leather jackets, fists in the air and foaming pints of ale in the air. Later outside that night's venue 'The Tabor', Marvin glanced up at the cinema style board of the club during load-in and mumbled "Oh for fuck's sake!" Everyone looked up and laughter broke out as the billboard read K.S.U.K.

STARVED AND DELIRIOUS, TOXIC NARCOTIC, SWINGIN' UTTERS and CHAOS U.K. played to a half empty house and they apparently had female dancers join in. I say apparently as I had my first night off after a fight with a Bloody Mary and crashed out in the van. Pig champion turned up looking slimmer and a fracas occurred at a 7-11 after a punk rock shoplifting incident got ugly, and of course the cops turned up.

Friday August the 12th came around and I got up early as I always do and hit the shower. I came out to find everyone had bailed and left me at Ty's house to entertain myself while they all went to Pig Champion's place. Apparently he talked about the old days, showed them the first POISON IDEA practice room in his basement and revealed to them his plans for how he saw his last stand, to die in a hotel room dealing drugs with maids looking after his every need.

They finally came back in the late afternoon to a pissed off Welly and gave me a sealed factory cassette of the Ian MacKaye EP as a consolation prize. Later we ended up in a bar again and then headed over to Todd Norin from THE UNAMUSED's house for a short-lived party, but most of us were too tired to fully get into proceedings.

CHAPTER 27: SHUT UP, I'LL DO THE TALKING

On the following day of Saturday the 13th of August it was decided that it was pointless trying to get to that night's gig in Denver, Colorado, as it was 1240 miles away (great tour planning part three), so we drove east then south east through Boise, Idaho, until eventually we gave up and pulled over late at night into the Perry Rest Area near the Great Salt Lake in Northern Utah. Pat and myself tried sleeping on the benches surrounding one of the shelters until 5am when the sun started to come up and the sprinklers came on and soaked us, so we moved to different benches on the hexagonal shelter. Then a different set of sprinklers came on and so on until we finally gave up.

We commenced driving again as dawn broke through the barren mountainous terrain, and no sooner had we started driving than we were pulled over by the highway patrol at 7am on Sunday the 14th of August somewhere in Northern Utah. "Shut up, I'll do the talking", mumbled Vic as the cop approached the vehicle, but somehow he blagged it, a pair of smoking motorcycle boots were all that remained on the remote stretch of highway as we drove away.

Lawrence, Kansas, was impossible to reach from our location, so it also had to be wiped from the itinerary (great tour planning part four), and after driving most of the day we found ourselves in a scenic spot somewhere in the Rockies, at a trader outpost with a carving of a clown outside, phoning every upcoming gig promoter to warn of the tour promoters rip-off ways.

A guy called Mike Kelly (a.k.a. Mike Mosher among other assumed names) was at this time based in S.F. (later New Orleans, apparently his hometown) where he ran an outfit called I.T.P. Now word down the wire was that he had been messing tours up for bands, ripping off promoters and the bands, before doing a runner to a new hideout as well as giving the bands a bad name. He'd pulled out of this tour

during the Southern California leg but had phoned all
upcoming promoters and told them that CHAOS U.K. wanted
an extra $500 to be wired directly to him. Some promoters
pulled out and some sent him money (which the band never
saw). He apparently left S.F. the day before CHAOS U.K.
arrived and was never heard from again. So Marvin bought
a phone card and employed his gift of the gab, managing
to convince most of the promoters that he was telling the
truth, and saved the day for a lot of the upcoming dates.

As a result of the impossible distances we passed through
Denver a day late that evening, and the promoter was kind
enough to offer us free tickets to see THE OFFSPRING, who
were now apparently big news, but Uncle Dad and Ruprecht
up front (Vic and Gabba) wouldn't allow it. Bored of BLACK
SABBATH tapes Gabba put the radio on and a song came on,
the latest smash hit apparently, and over the road rumble
the band sounded familiar, with some kid singing about
having the time to listen to him whine. Little did we know.

We drove on and stopped at a roadside motel outside Limon,
Colorado, got cold cans of pop from the loud vending
machines, piled into the wood-panelled room and laughed at
the Gideon's Bibles in the bedside cabinets while trying
to find something to watch on the antiquated wooden TV.

On the following day of Monday August the 15th, we drove
again but alas St. Louis, Missouri had to be abandoned
as it was over 750 miles away, so we drove and drove and
everyone began to lose their minds. Again, we stopped at a
motel somewhere on the Kansas/Nebraska State line before
finally three days after leaving Portland, nearly 1900
miles away, we arrived in Omaha a day early.

It was Tuesday August the 16th and there was nothing to
do on the plains under the leaden sky of Nebraska, so we
went to the 'Capitol Bar' at 1011 Capitol Avenue a whole
day early and met up with ska all-stars INSATIABLE from
Salt Lake City and THE PIETASTERS from Washington D.C.

who were playing that night. They seemed friendly so we stuck around and skanked the night away with the Colonel and the Devilman getting wasted at the long bar adjacent to the band room. Afterwards we stayed at local promoter Kathleen's house and then spent the next day of Wednesday the 17th of August looking around this pleasant quiet town and record shopping at Drastic Plastic, where I found the STRETCH MARKS LP on BYO before we all wolfed down all you can eat pasta and headed to the gig back at the Capitol.

We got to the club to find out that the SWINGIN' UTTERS had made it but TOXIC NARCOTIC hadn't. We found out later that they'd left Portland earlier than everyone else and made it to the Lawrence and St. Louis gigs, but hadn't known anymore of the dates after that and had thought everyone else had given up due to our no shows. We didn't see them for a while. CHAOS U.K. ripped it up in fine style in Omaha, and partied all night long.

PAT

CHAPTER 28: MINNEAPOLICE

On Thursday August the 18th the road headed north for six hours to Minneapolis. We rolled up late and were met by the charmingly named Pig Nose and Red Skull of ASSRASH who escorted us on their motorcycles in their cut-off jackets, shorts and biker boots, like a scene from a Mid-West Mad Max in the leafy suburbs of Minnesota. After dropping off our bags at the MISERY/ASSRASH house at 3629 Aldrich Avenue South we headed over to their local, the C.C. Motorcycle Club Bar before being eaten alive by mosquitoes in their basement for the night.

On the following day of Friday August the 19th we went back to the bar again, visited Extreme Noise Records, and then to the gig at 'Dremly Studios' at 504 Cedar Avenue, put on by Extreme Noise and Havoc Records. A boiling hot warehouse packed to the rafters with no air conditioning and no-one allowed back in if they went outside. At some point I gave up and went for a walk to cool off and ended up at the Mississippi River, looking over at St. Paul. ASSRASH, MISERY and the SWINGIN' UDDERS (sic) played another great set before CHAOS U.K. took to the stage to a full house of inebriated nutcases who loved every minute of it.

After the gig we headed back to the ASSRASH house and our gracious hosts rustled up an after-gig party at the house on Aldrich Avenue. It was getting late and I wanted to grab something to eat so I went for a five minute walk to a local gas station around the corner at West 36th and South Lyndale. On the way back a cop car started following me and slowly crawled behind. "Shit!" I knew what happened next after being put up against a police car for being punk after dark a few years before.

I stepped it up a bit to try and get back to the house before they could stop me, I looked back as I was turning the corner onto Aldrich Avenue and they were speeding up, so after I turned the corner I broke into a run. Luckily I

had the key to the van and somehow I managed to unlock it,
jump in, re-lock it, and hide myself under a sleeping bag
behind the back row of seats in seconds, frozen.

"Come out, we know you're in there". "Fuck, they must've
seen me get in". I didn't move I just lay there motionless,
minimising my breathing for what felt like an hour as
they scanned and re-scanned the inside of the van with
their flashlights, repeatedly calling me out. Luckily they
gave up after five to ten minutes and I heard muted voices
coming from the house, "Welly, Welly, come in." I didn't
move, I wasn't sure. The voices continued and eventually
I peered out to see that the cops had gone and I returned
to the party which was now a house full of punks sat in
complete silence with all the lights off. Whenever I think
of Minneapolis I think of cops.

I needed some sleep after this so Chaos and I headed over to
Sid from MISERY and his partner Cricket's house as they'd
offered to put some of us up. They lived in a nearby suburb
and we got a chance to get some shut-eye in a quiet house
before they took us to a local greasy spoon the following
morning of Saturday the 20th of August. While there they
struck up a conversation with someone on the table behind
us and it turned out to be Lori Barbero of BABES IN TOYLAND
who explained to them that she'd missed the gig the night
before due to a book launch for 'BABES IN TOYLAND: The
Making and Selling of a Rock and Roll Band' by Neal Karlen.

Back at the ASSRASH motel everyone was still in the same
seats out of their minds and grinding their teeth. The
Devilman had gone AWOL the night before, no one knew where
he was and nobody had a mobile phone for a few years yet.
Disappointingly, talk turned to going to a 'titty bar'
and most of the males in attendance left in excitement,
jumping in the back of a pick-up truck for some base ape
entertainment. Above all that sort of thing I opted to stay
at the ranch with the females of the punk house and scowled
in disgust in my black militaristic attire.

Marvin hadn't slept since Omaha and I have no idea how but we later ended up at a party with these teen punk kids in attendance. It turned out that they were apparently the Toulon brothers from the band OLD SKULL from Madison, Wisconsin, J.P. and Jamie. They were nine and ten years old when they formed in 1989, splitting up in 1993, making them 14 and 15 years old and out of their not very old skulls at a Minneapolis punk squat party. After the party fizzled out we returned to the ASSRASH punk house and crashed out.

CHAPTER 29: THE WENDY'S INCIDENT

We waved farewell to ASSRASH and the Twin Cities and headed for Chicago on Sunday the 21st of August. A brief stop off at a Wendy's eating establishment somewhere en route saw the Colonel reassert his punk rock credentials by sneering and intentionally farting loudly to piss off the locals. Gambling on a fart after that much vodka and Taco Bell was never going to pay off and after a quick sprint to 'the John' to clean up we were back on the tarmac singing him a puerile tour song based on a BEACH BOYS classic, "Wendy's - the Colonel nearly followed through, Wendy's - he gambled on a number two, Wendy's - he didn't get a second chance, Wendy's - the Colonel nearly shit his pants." The van filled with laughter apart from the grumbling Colonel in the back, "Eeeasy as you go Le Taff et le Taff Deux (Marv and Welly) or you will feel the back of a sailor's hand" he chided.

Six hours of relentless toilet related piss-taking later we were at the 'Fireside Bowl' at 2646 West Fullerton Avenue in Chicago. Yes it was a punk gig in a bowling alley, Hardcore Happy Days. THE MUSHUGANAS played their SCREECHING WEASEL style punk, SWINGIN' UTTERS tore it up big style, we met THE BOLLWEEVILS, and then it was CHAOS U.K.'s turn.

There were a few over enthusiastic young punks in attendance and one guy kept getting on stage and fucking with the equipment, grabbing the microphone and being a general pain in the arse. Chaos finally got sick of it after getting the microphone smacked into his teeth and handed the young upstart a little corporal punishment. The rest of the set was relatively uneventful apart from the fact that this was all going on side-on to bowling lanes and we kept expecting Chachi and Richie to show up for a rumble.

We sat in the Fireside Bowl bar afterwards and both CHAOS U.K. and SWINGIN' UTTERS were video interviewed before a few of us headed to their friends' Karl and Rob from IMPULSE MANSLAUGHTER's house for some rest and recreation.

We were getting to know the SWINGIN' UTTERS by this point and a friendlier bunch of punks you couldn't wish to meet. Johnny the vocalist was like a slightly less drunk and more reserved Shane MacGowan, Max on guitar was the Liberty spiked punk, ex-Marine and the businessman of the band, while other guitarist Darius was the sharp song writer of Scandinavian descent who wanted a Viking burial, Kevin Wickersham on the bass was quiet but smart and a teacher, while Greg on the drums was the hard partying rude boy with an Upsetter Records tattoo running up his forearm.

At the IMPULSE MANSLAUGHTER house Marvin had an unhinged meltdown as he'd been awake since Omaha that went something like, "Look, just fuckin' (bang!) shit, don't... twat, (slam!) FUCK! It's... bollocks! Shit, I just wanna go to fucking sleep!" And finally, finally, he hit the land of nod.

We'd left Chaos and the Devilman the night before to the evils of vodka, so the following day of Monday August the 22nd we met them at a bar but they had no intention of stopping, so Marvin, Vic, Gabba and myself met up with Rob, his friend Lemmy, a German black metaller, and a guy simply called 'the Mouth'. We were taken to Lake Michigan where Gabba, Vic and myself ended up on a small boat on the lake drifting further and further away from the shore, the skyline becoming a vague outline on the horizon, and as the sun went down we raised our red plastic cups full of American beer and toasted like pirates of the high seas.

Once ashore we headed back to Rob and Karl's place and their huge pet Iguana that we accidentally let out by leaving the front door open and then had to rescue it out of a tree. They had a collection of VHS punk video compilations and to our surprise a lot of them were crust bands that had been filmed in both Marv and my hometown of Cardiff at gigs Marv had put on that I'd made the flyers for circa 1988. After being suitably amused by gigs from six years previous we all gradually fell unconscious after a hard day messing about on the lake.

CHAPTER 30: WE'RE NOT INDUSTRIAL, WE'RE AGRICULTURAL!

On Tuesday the 23rd of August we said goodbye to Karl and Rob and drove through strange lands for four hours to Muncie, Indiana, and it started to feel like we were on the edge of the world. We walked in and it was dark and the gig was practically empty with a few kids sitting around in what looked like a community centre. Judging by some of the t-shirts there appeared to be African American white power skinheads in attendance, and some oddball started rambling to me unsolicited about 'post-neo-industrial comic books' or some shit so I talked unintelligible bollocks back at him and he wandered back off.

To top off the strange vibe of the gig, after his two day vodka binge in Chicago, Chaos was on his death bed in the back of the van looking more than a little jaundiced. He wouldn't or couldn't move and all he was saying was "I... can't... do... it", so it was decided to cart him off somewhere quiet to die, so we just drove off. It was a strange feeling, I remember looking out of the window at these bemused kids wondering where the band were going. For our sins we ended up lost and sat in the dark in a clearing between some trees next to a grain silo, and illuminated by floodlights to the sound of one hundred thousand crickets singing to the late-night Mid-West humidity, we unfolded a map on the van hood to figure out where the closest, cheapest, worst motel in Indiana was located.

On the following day of Wednesday the 24th August, another four hours was spent driving past and through the end of the world and into outer space, also known as Detroit. Behold the wasteland. The venue, the 'Falcon Club' at 3515 Caniff Street in Hamtramck, a city within Detroit, was an old Polish night spot judging by the eagle motif over the door, all brick wall and austere with the atmosphere of a mortuary, even all the windows were bricked up. This cold and dark venue these days is a Super Discounts store, on this night though it was skinhead night.

After some free pizza and cheap beer (hey, what's new?) we noticed some Skrewdriver Boneheads policing the joint. The SWINGIN' UTTERS went down like a big ol' flaming bag of shite and so did THE BEERWHORES (and they knew the fucking skinheads), and following that CHAOS U.K. didn't manage to redeem the evening's entertainment.

On reflection the night was the closest I'd ever felt to being in a dystopian movie, the skins intimidated the entire crowd and the place had an atmosphere not unlike a freezer. Afterwards we ended up at a guy from CIVIL DISOBEDIENCE house with all this alien stuff everywhere and we slept in the loft, Chaos found a box of dodgy mags and we got out of there pronto in the morning.

On Thursday August the 25th we drove back out of the edge of the world, through the middle of nowhere and after a reasonably short three hour jaunt around the edge of Lake Erie we ended up in Cleveland's the 'Grog Shop' at 2785 Euclid Heights Boulevard, for some punk 'n' roll where SWINGIN' UTTERS and CHAOS U.K. played good sets to a small but enthusiastic audience, and afterwards we ended up staying at some 'I wannabe in the mafia' tough guy's house.

CHAPTER 31: CHILDREN OF THE CORNDOGS

On Friday the 26th of August some of us swapped vehicles,
I jumped in the SWINGIN' UTTERS station wagon and they put
a tape on of the new RANCID demo they'd been telling me
about. It sounded different to their earlier stuff even
though I couldn't hear much as the rumble was really loud
in the back of the truck and I told them it sounded like
RANCID were now trying to copy the SWINGIN' UTTERS style.
It turned out to be the demo for 'And Out Come the Wolves'.

We floored it through yet more weird country roads until we
hit the 'Hotel Evergreen', a few miles south of Edinboro
University on Route 99 in Edinboro, North West Pennsylvania,
for a two day punk festival called the 'Wall Of Sound'.
CHAOS U.K. were headlining the first night but not before
multitudes of bands from all over, but mostly Pittsburgh,
were due to play all day and all night.

The hotel was like a dilapidated wreck in the middle
of cornfields, a Salem's Lot meets Children of the Corn-
looking building that was home to approximately eight
million flies. There were a few dozen or so punks in a field
getting eaten alive by mosquitoes and the promoter was in
his forties and obviously into punk rock as opposed to
money. The bands were as follows, some didn't play but
here's a run down of day one as advertised; ABALIENATION,
THE ADDICTS, ANTI-FLAG, DOC HOPPER, LARRY BRRRDS, MY THREE
SCUM, RAIL, WALKING WITH EDNA, and CHAOS U.K.

Our time there was fun and CHAOS U.K. played to an
enthusiastic crowd like the anti-heroes they were, and
the rest of the night was spent talking with a variety of
bands and punks around various fires in the field near the
tree line, especially Marvin and the Devilman who for some
reason talked the lugholes off anyone within earshot.

We left Punk Rock Salem's Lot early on Saturday August the
27th for the long nine hour haul to Boston. As a result

we completely missed day two of the festival and I was
disappointed because THE MEATMEN headlined, but the rest
of the bands were; ABNEGATION, BROTHER'S KEEPER, DUMPSTER
JUICE, THE FIGGS, ICU, POP SICKLE, PUNCH BUGGY, SHADES
APART, SINKHOLE, and SWINGIN' UTTERS, who later bought
me a 'We're the Meatmen' shirt from Tesco himself as a
consolation prize. The downside to the festival was we
heard that at the end of the second day a kid stage dived
to THE MEATMEN and broke his neck. We also later heard that
he never walked again and his parents sued the promoter.

We stopped briefly to visit Niagara Falls after driving 135
miles towards Boston, and watched blue and yellow lemmings
make their way down the rock faces and jump into boats
and float off into the mist. Marvin started to hallucinate
at one point shouting, "LOG! VIC! There's a log in front
of us!" There was no log on the road in front of us... he
hadn't slept again. The Devilman acquired a tooth abscess
en route and his face changed shape, horns sprouted and much
groaning ensued until we hit Boston at 4am the following
morning and rudely awoke TOXIC NARCOTIC at their punk house
and piled in to sleep the few remaining hours of the night.

On the following day of Sunday August the 28th the Ganzini
Brothers (Marvin and the Devilman) went for a check up
at the hospital before hitting the gig at 'Axis' on 15
Lansdowne Street next to Fenway Park in Boston just as
TOXIC NARCOTIC were finishing their set. We talked to them
before the SWINGIN' UTTERS played really well to a packed
house at this plush rock club and then CHAOS U.K. ripped
through their songs to a similar reception. Loads of free
Budweiser was commandeered before leaving the early finish
gig at 8:30pm for the TOXIC NARCOTIC house on a leafy
street somewhere in the suburbs, and a keg party in their
basement. We were joined by loads of fun loving Bostonians
who drank from red cups and then promptly left as soon as
the keg was empty. Only the diehard remained, including
us, TOXIC NARCOTIC, and a one Paul Bearer of SHEER TERROR
who cracked jokes as we partied into the early hours.

CHAPTER 32: ANOTHER RELIGION, ANOTHER TOUR

On Monday August the 29th we hit the road back to New York for five hours, even though it was only just over 200 miles, to 'ABC-No-Rio', a small ex-art gallery that kept its name but had turned into a punk venue. The ground floor was a DIY punk rock supermarket run by Neil of Tribal War and the basement was the venue, a tiny spray-painted dive. Outside, the pavement was full of gutter punks and rodents, you would've walked past the place and never realised you had.

First up was ABALIENATION with their version of 'At The Hop' altered to 'Let's Kill A Cop', then it was the SWINGIN' UTTERS turn and slowly people started to come down to watch. PUBLIC NUISANCE filled the place and heckled the locals as much as they heckled them, much messing around in the form of mock metal covers and tomfoolery proceeded and they didn't play my favourite song 'Cheap Sex and Booze'.

CHAOS U.K. went down as you would expect, raucous fucking rock with drunken punks throwing themselves off the walls, but when THE VARUKERS started playing, water started running down the aforementioned walls and onto the gear. I saw sparks and smoke, saw what was coming, and climbed up the ladder to the ground floor and headed outside. Dodgy electrics paranoia coupled with claustrophobia cleared the place in minutes, THE VARUKERS set was cut short and the final gig of the tour was over. We said farewell to Will and Amy of the TOXIC NARCOTIC crew and headed off to Val and Polly's apartment for our four remaining days in N.Y.C.

When we got there Vic kicked us out of the van and unleashed eight weeks of stress in fifteen minutes with his girlfriend. Then the van and trailer was cleared of all our shit in the middle of the street at 3am and a passing pedestrian decided to help himself to Gabba's suitcase. This was quickly retrieved and the thief was told to fuck off before we climbed flights and flights of stairs, lugging everything we had before we could finally rest.

Tuesday the 30th of August was spent ridding ourselves of the last of our money down St. Marks and on Broadway, and then evenings of relaxation with Val and Polly, Julian and Jimmy of PUBLIC NUISANCE, and Greg of MAGGOT.

On Wednesday the 31st of August we arranged to meet the SWINGIN' UTTERS at Mona's Bar for the final session of all sessions, but only the Colonel and I could muster the energy so he donned his two-tone ska suit that came courtesy of THE PIETASTERS and we drank and chatted to SWINGIN' UTTERS and various VARUKERS and SUICIDAL SUPERMARKET TROLLEYS. Later we hung around outside while punks messed with cockroaches and everyone fell home sideways in the small hours.

The following day was Thursday September the 1st, and after 12,000 road miles across 35 States, it was over. We met up with Vic and ex-GBH Joe at the airport for a final farewell. The flight seemed a hell of a lot longer on the way back but soon enough we were descending through the clouds into the sullen grey of South East England. I gazed out of the window at the miniature cars and thought to myself that I'd like to do it all again one day, but next time I'd like to do it with the band I was in, FOUR LETTER WORD.

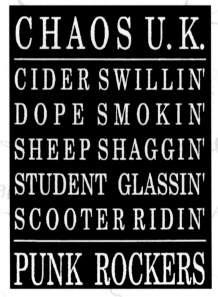

THE TOUR T-SHIRT: 'BUD DWYER' FRONT AND 'NIRVANA' BACK

TOXIC NARCOTIC

POPULUTION: FALLOUT SHELTER

CHAOS U.K

LOUD, POLITICAL AND UNCOMPROMISING: RENO

CHAOSUK

AIRBORNE IN EUGENE

$WINGIN' UTTER$

TEENAGE GENOCIDE AT THE OFF RAMP

CHAOS U.K

SECRET MEN IN SEATTLE

KSUK AT THE TABOR, PORTLAND

Pietasters

BRINGING THE SKA TO OMAHA

CHAOS U.K

RONNIE WAS A REBEL IN OMAHA

MISERY

SID IN MINNEAPOLIS

MISERY

JON AT THE DREMLY STUDIOS

HARDCORE HAPPY DAYS, CHICAGO

LIVE AT THE FIRESIDE BOWL

CHICAGO: OUTSKIRTS OF TOWN

YO-HO: WELLY, VIC & GABBA ON LAKE MICHIGAN

CHAOS U.K.

HEAD ON A POLE AT THE GROG SHOP, CLEVELAND

PUNK ROCK SALEM'S LOT, EDINBORO, PA

SETTING UP THE WALL OF SOUND

CHAOS U.K

EARSLAUGHTER IN EDINBORO, PA

POSING AT NIAGARA FALLS

DISCHORD SHOOT: NIAGARA FALLS

CHAOS U.K

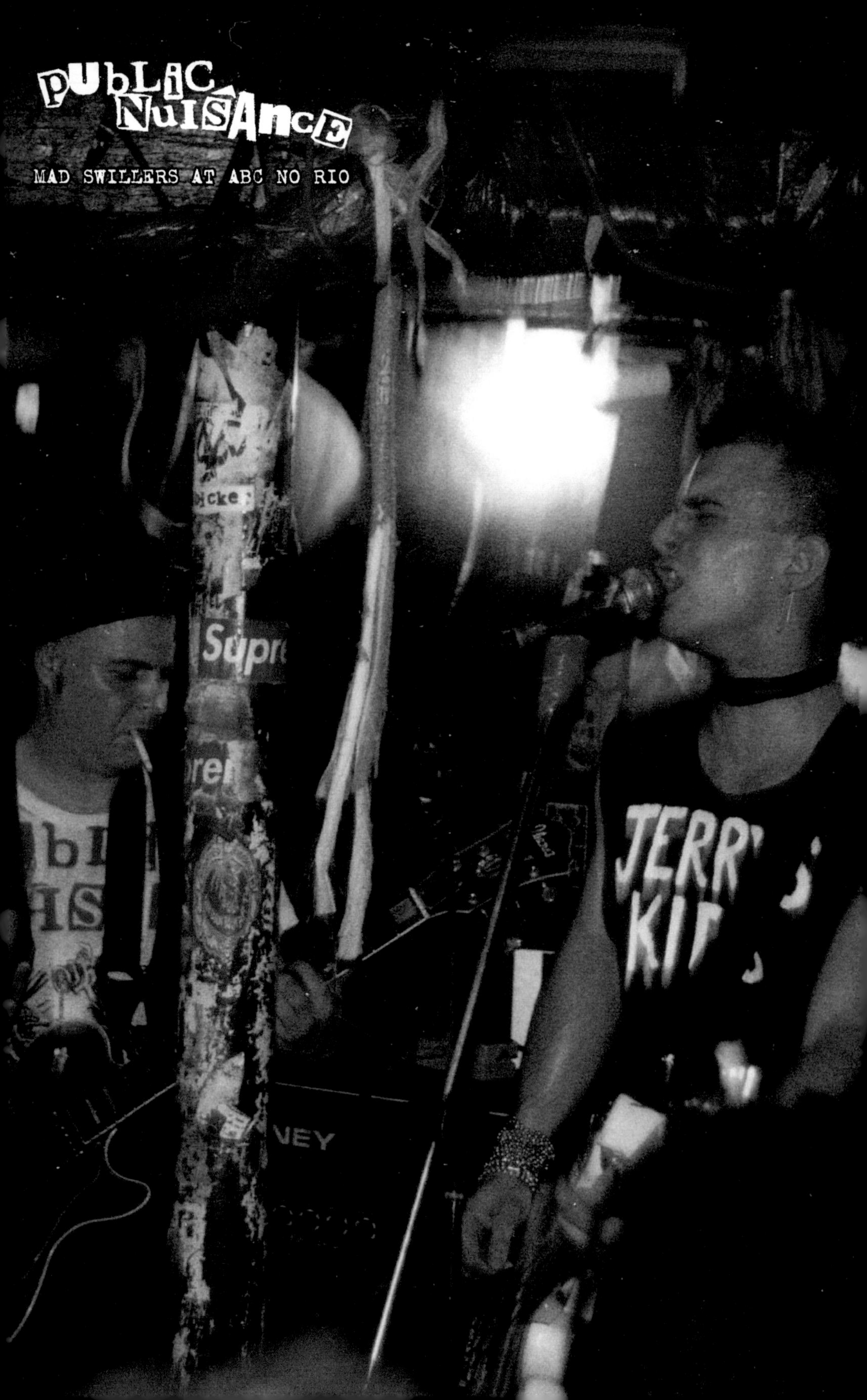
PUBLIC NUISANCE
MAD SWILLERS AT ABC NO RIO

CROWD SHOT AT THE ABC

KEV AND RAT VARUKER AT MONA'S
INSET: VIC, CHRISTINE, RAT, WELLY, KEV & PAT AT THE ABC

CHAOS AND DARIUS SAY GOODBYE AT MONA'S

CHAOS IN HIS SKA SUIT

THE UTTERS AND FRIEND AT MONA'S BAR, NEW YORK

CHAOS U.K. - HOPE YOU GOT A FUCKIN' HEADACHE TOUR 1994

Sunday 10th July - New York, NY - Wetlands
Tuesday 12th July - Providence, RI - Club Babyhead
Wednesday 13th July - Philadelphia, PA - Firenze
Thursday 14th July - Richmond, VA - Factory
Friday 15th July - Hampton, VA - N-Sect Club
Saturday 16th July - Atlanta, GA - Sombre Reptile
Sunday 17th July - Daytona Beach, FL - Black Eyed Susan's
Monday 18th July - Davie, Fl - Plus Five Club
Tuesday 19th July - Tampa, FL - Stone Lounge
Thursday 21st July - Gainesville, FL - Hardback Cafe
Friday 22nd July - New Orleans, LA - Bridge Lounge
Saturday 23rd July - Houston, TX - Harvey's Club Deluxe
Sunday 24th July - Austin, TX - Liberty Lunch
Monday 25th July - Dallas, TX - Galaxy Club
Friday 29th July - San Diego, CA - SOMA
Saturday 30th July - Capistrano Beach, CA - Doheny Saloon
Sunday 31st July - San Clemente, CA - Skate Ramp Party
Tuesday 2nd August - Los Angeles, CA - Chapalitas
Wednesday 3rd August - Corona, CA - Showcase Theatre
Thursday 4th August - Long Beach, CA - Golden Sails Hotel
Friday 5th August - San Jose, CA - Cactus Club
Saturday 6th August - Santa Barbara, CA - The Underground
Sunday 7th August - Berkeley, CA - 924 Gilman
Monday 8th August - Reno, NV - Fallout Shelter
Tuesday 9th August - Eugene, OR - WOW Hall
Wednesday 10th August - Seattle, WA - Off Ramp
Thursday 11th August - Portland, OR - Tabor
Wednesday 17th August - Omaha, NB - Capitol Bar
Friday 19th August - Minneapolis, MN - Dremly Studios
Sunday 21st August - Chicago, IL - Fireside Bowl
Wednesday 24th August - Hamtranck, MI - Falcon Club
Thursday 25th August - Cleveland, OH - Grog Shop
Friday 26th August - Edinboro, PA - Wall of Sound Festival
Sunday 28th August - Boston, MA - Axis
Monday 29th August - New York, NY - ABC-No-Rio

TYPICAL CHAOS U.K. 1994 SET LIST

Bodies (SEX PISTOLS)
Ronnie Was A Rebel I+II
Kill Your Baby
For Adolfs' Only (VALVES)
Cider I Up Landlord
Kill (ALBERTOS Y LOST TRIOS PARANOIAS)
Ramraid
Head On A Pole
Army
Selfish Few
Four Minute Warning
Wall Street Crash
Police Story (PARTISANS)
Government Nears
Secret Men
Brainbomb (PUNISHMENT OF LUXURY)
No Security
Happy Spastic
Student
A Swindle
Farmyard Boogie
Victimised
Sunday Morning Nightmare (SHAM 69)
Degenerated (REAGAN YOUTH)

R Dear MaximumRocknRoll:

I am writing this letter in order for this to be made public to expose a bunch of retarded swindling egocentric sexual perverts. After Chaos U.K. played my hometown at Black Eyed Susans on the 7/17/94, extending my good nature and hospitality. By inviting the band back to stay at my parents' house while my father was away on business. The evening started in good spirits until the point where two bottles of vodka, endless six packs and large quantities of pot were produced from their tour coach. Gradually their mood became more and more intense due to their argument between the singer and drummer over the last can of beer. As if this wasn't enough their clown of a guitarist produced a bag of crack cocaine and a tin of carpet adhesive. This was consumed by various members of the band over the next half hour and acted as a catalyst for the ensuing destruction.

The first act of idiocy was the continuation of the argument between singer/drummer which resulted in glasses bein' thrown across my living room. My friend tried to calm things down and the guitarist attacked my friend with a poker. During the scuffle the singer and drummer turned their attention from each other to me and my friends, as this was happening I heard a scream from upstairs as the bass player had urinated on the landing and proceeded to remove his clothing and tried to get into bed with my mother. When I attempted to remove him from my mother's bedroom he insisted that I was being unreasonable as he claimed that my mother was "up to it".

At this point my mother phoned the police. The band found out and decided on one final spree of destruction: 1/ Fish tank broken by flying bottle; 2/ My records got destroyed; 3/ A door was ripped off it's hinges; 4/ Beer was poured on my comic collection; 5/ Soiled cat litter was scattered around the kitchen; 6/ Punctured my couch with screwdrivers.

Their last action was to punch me in the face before fleeing in their tour coach. As a result of this my mother is considering legal action and wants me out of the house.

I think its disgusting that people who pretend to care act with such hypocrisy. They do nothing but put a slur on our scene's reputation. Surely something can be done about these people before they abuse somebody else and take advantage of good natured people within the punk community. Green Day never behaved this way, so why should Chaos U.K. Yours in solidarity,
Ken Barlow

J Dear MRR,

This is in response to Ken Barlow's letter in Issue #137 about Chaos UK doing drugs and wrecking his home. On 7/29/94 Chaos UK stayed at my house. Sure, there were a few beers floating around and there was some marijuana consumption. But on the contrary, they were well behaved guests.

Victor, the guitar player, raked and mowed my lawn. Chaos was making cookies and pies while the Devil Man (drums) cleaned and mopped my kitchen, as well as cleaning my cat box and taking out the trash. Marvin the Sheep Shagger (bass) was washing my car and walked my elderly neighbors' dogs. Gabba was babysitting my nephew and even changed his diapers three times.

When I offered to give them some extra money for their help, they refused. So the next afternoon, I took them to see a matinee of *The Lion King*. After the film, they had to leave for their next show, and they gave my wife, Nancy, and I a lovely bouquet of roses.

I really hope they come back soon; my house could use a coat of paint. Thanks, guys.
Jim Martin, Malachi Krunch/Broken c/o Stinky Twinkie/ PO Box 1271/ New Haven, CT 06505

PS. When Green Day came around, they beat up peace punks outside the gig.

CHAOS U.K. TOUR ROUTE MAP 1994

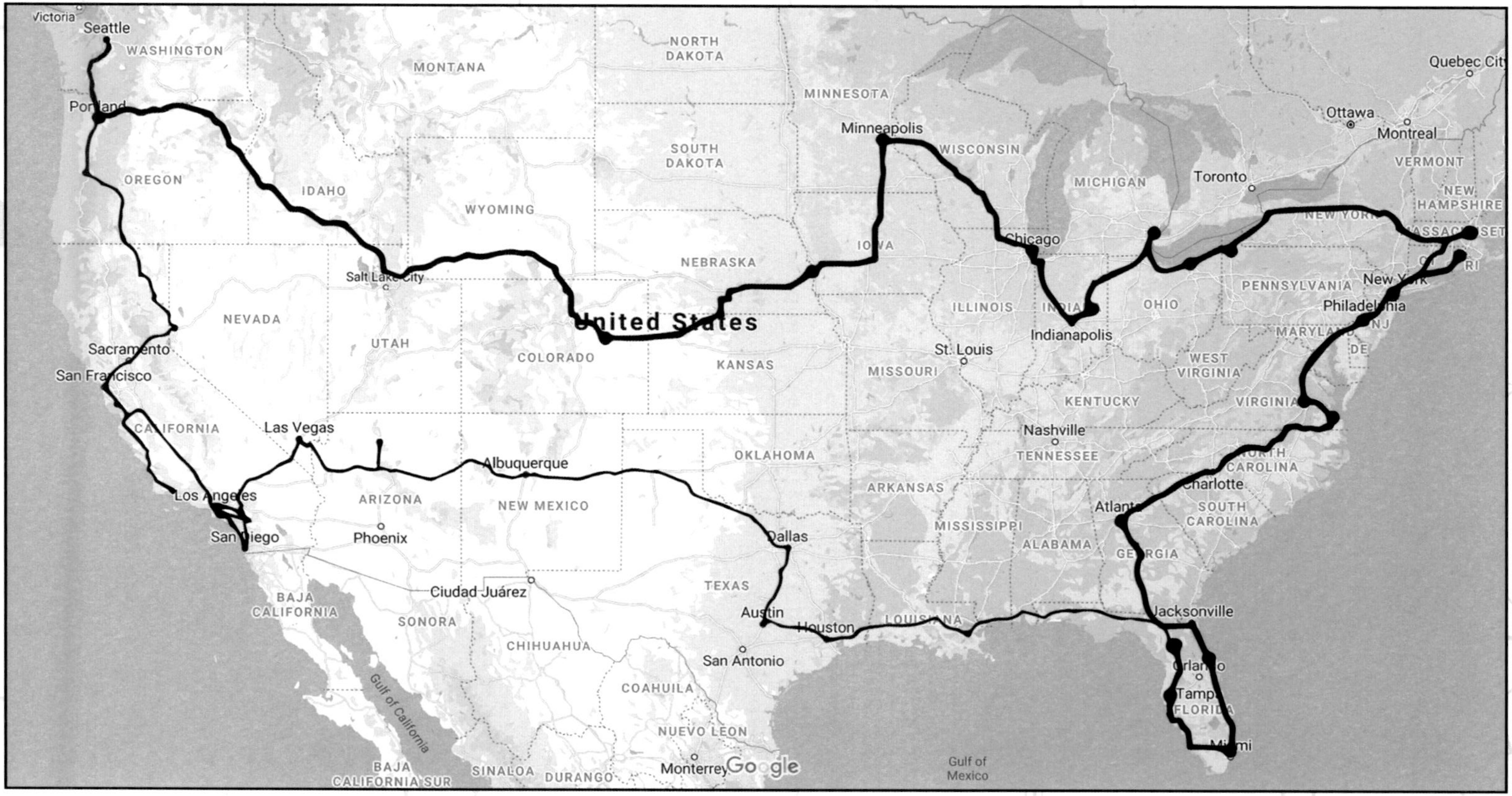

In the intervening years my better half and I had a son in 1995 around the same time as the band I was in, FOUR LETTER WORD, co-released our first 7" with Blackpool label J.S.N.T.G.M. Records. I'd been in touch with B.Y.O. a.k.a. the Better Youth Organization for a number of years and had interviewed Shawn Stern in 1991. B.Y.O. was one of my favourite labels so when the pressing was nearly sold out I decided to send him a copy just to see what he thought.

The phone rang one day and it was Shawn and he told me that they'd be interested in putting out our album. After my head stopped spinning of course we agreed, signing with them for three albums. They wanted us to work with an engineer who understood punk and asked Andy Turner formerly of the INSTIGATORS for recommendations. The name Frankie Stubbs was mentioned and Shawn asked if I knew LEATHERFACE, I replied that I had all their records. I was given a phone number and contacted Frankie about the recording. As a result we released our first album A Nasty Piece Of Work in 1997 and B.Y.O. booked a U.S. and Canadian tour to promote it in the summer of 1998. The night before we were due to fly to Los Angeles, we had a gig at 'The Garage' in London with STRUNG OUT on Saturday June the 20th...

CHAPTER 33: STRUNG OUT IN THE GARAGE

It was all arranged; the plane tickets were bought, the currency was exchanged, the jobs were left behind, and the bags were packed. All that was left was to say goodbye to our loved ones, organise a van to London for the gig the night before (and get it back without us), and find somewhere to stay. All seem simple enough? No chance.

So after waving goodbye to the entire band DOUG who'd turned up at my flat to see us all off, and the difficult task of parting company with my young son Kieran for two months, we wedged ourselves into a tiny clapped out ex-postal van along with girlfriends, pals and our hired hippie driver, and trundled painfully along the M4 in the rare searing heat of a cloudless British afternoon in early summer.

A few hours later the claustrophobic sardine tin became too much when we came to a standstill in traffic outside Harrods in a gridlocked Knightsbridge and were taking turns to breath through a tiny hole in the partition, so half of us alighted and opted for the tube train to Highbury Corner and 'The Garage'. We hopped back off the tube and arrived at the same time as the tinned sardines who traversed the London traffic to park at the back door and load in.

The soundcheck was over in no time as the house P.A. sounded great so we ran over the road and slammed a couple of pints before playing the opening slot at 8:30pm. The humid club filled as we played and by the end of the set we were playing to about 350 people in the shadows beyond the stage barrier. A good crowd response was gratefully accepted by us humble Welsh amateurs and even a few dared to skank to an opening band, which was rare.

Next up a U.S. band called WHIPPERSNAPPER played their 90s California by numbers, before STRUNG OUT played and just sounded and acted like a metal band, only entering the venue to play their set. We spent the rest of the evening next to our merch table watching the bank of Fat Wreck Chords count wads of cash while we sold one CD and a 7".

I prised our measly fifty quid pay out of the promoter before driving to Camberwell with our friends Brit and Marie to stay at their flat. Jon's girlfriend wept like a grieving grandmother before falling out of the back of the van onto her backside in a drunken stupor, Jon quickly running into the house to avoid further embarrassment, while the rest of us carried out more dignified farewells and waved the van off before eating Pot Noodles and passing out, dreaming of our unknown futures in strange foreign climes.

CHAPTER 34: WHAT ARE YOU GUYS DOOOING?

After an excellent breakfast courtesy of our hosts on Sunday the 21st of June, we said goodbye and headed off on a succession of tube trains to Victoria Station and clambered onto the Heathrow tube, laughing at the busker who'd had the great idea of forcing a captive audience to listen to him while locked in a moving train.

We checked in and boarded our Air New Zealand flight with no time to spare except for some hurried duty free purchases. The flight took off promptly and was fairly uneventful, the only highlight being that we received the correct veggie and vegan meals before falling asleep. Ten or so hours later we descended through the orange smog haze of early evening Los Angeles and into LAX Airport.

We entered immigration clutching our forms containing the addresses of people who worked at B.Y.O. Records for our first night in the U.S. This went without a hitch but then Hairy seemed to think "We're in!" and went about putting everyone's bags onto the same trolley before we'd even got as far as the customs guards.

A few rapid eyeball movements were exchanged before we all grabbed our own bags and walked towards customs separately, then four out of five of us were waved towards large uniformed gentlemen wearing rubber gloves. I managed to get my officer onto the subject of work and he eased up and became chatty before letting me and the others pass, including Will, who'd been waving his 'pen pal' André Duguay's address in a guard's face in an eighteen year old style panic, but somehow he blagged it.

We headed straight through the main exit of LAX that was in front of us and out into the dry heat of Los Angeles, and the smokers among us chain smoked for twenty minutes before the familiar face of Shawn Stern appeared looking agitated, "What are you guys doooing? This is not the Air

New Zealand stand, this is the main entrance!" Feeling like scolded schoolboys we walked the twenty or so yards to the YOUTH BRIGADE van chatting with the mildly annoyed Shawn while the others followed, lugging their bags with their chins dragging on the floor.

Mark Stern was waiting in the van and I introduced everyone to the two brothers while they were all throwing their bags into the back of the mini-bus, "This is Jon, our guitarist". A tall dark stranger, economic with his words, but he used them wisely. "That's Hairy, he's the bassist". The opposite of Jon, a recent recruit, and already showing early signs of strange behaviour. "That guy over there is Will, he's the drummer". The newest addition and only just turned 18, quiet and insular. "And finally, this is Graham". Our friend from Bristol, who I'd invited along to give someone else the opportunity that I'd had in 1994.

After a short and confusing drive through Marina Del Rey listening to the Stern brothers argue about which was the best place to eat, we ended up at a small Mexican restaurant holding huge Burritos and cold bottles of Corona while getting to know our label bosses. Then we headed off to Shawn's new house on Sunset Avenue down on Venice Beach, where he had two half-built apartments on either side of a house he'd just bought and turned into a duplex. He showed us the empty half and we slept on anything we could find.

WORKING FOR THE YANKEE DOLLAR FROM THE ORIGINAL TOUR REPORT

CHAPTER 35: IF YOU DON'T SHOWER EVERY DAY

I woke up at 2am, 3am and finally 5am on Monday June the 22nd in a sweat-soaked jet lag hell, listening to the bus depot across Pacific Avenue through the half finished windows of Shawn's house. One by one we washed and shaved as best we could from a bucket of cold water with a shard of mirror like in an old Western, before visiting a deserted and grey Venice Beach in the early morning where we polished off omelettes and coffee at Café Venicia on the sea front.

While eating breakfast we'd talked about the World Cup that was apparently going on in other football curious parts of the world, so after our mugs were drained we headed back to Shawn's and Hairy managed to find a channel on the old black and white portable TV in Shawn's empty apartment that had a game on and we squinted at the distorted half tuned picture while England lost to Romania on Mexican TV with accompanying frantic commentary, "GOOOAAALLL!".

After his morning workout at Venice's Gold's Gym, Shawn drove us to the B.Y.O. offices to meet the rest of the label crew. While driving he sniffed a few times and imparted some local advice to us in his bass-baritone voice, "If you don't shower every day, you'll never get laid in L.A."

B.Y.O. was in Suite 4 in a small business estate at 4051 Glencoe Avenue in Marina Del Rey. Downstairs was the warehouse, toilet, and Mark Stern's office, upstairs was the bustling nerve centre with the main area housing Nick, Ron, André and Rory, and a separate area for Kris the office under manager. A little bit more separated from the hard working drones was Shawn's office from where he shouted "Buy!" and "Sell!" and "Let's do lunch!" through the intercom while throwing vast quantities of demo tapes into a large bin.

I answered a phone interview the label had set up for a paper called the Stockton Record while the others read zines and picked their noses in the reception area listening to music. After this we decided to hit the streets of Marina Del Rey and walked for hours in the searing Californian sun along dusty pavements only inches from certain death at the hands of crazed lunatics in high speed motor vehicles, all driving on the wrong side of the road.

We stumbled across a supermarket and jointly spent $40 on some supplies before what seemed like many more miles were hiked, but were probably just a few, before we finally reached Shawn's place and did what all British people do when abroad and drank beer. While cooking up a strange concoction of pasta and salsa many beers were quaffed while trying to get the building site tape player to work and Will was the only person who could manage to do it.

Shawn returned at 6pm from a hard day's slaving at the office and was instantly outraged that we weren't acting more like Californians, "Eewwww! What are you guys dooooin? I bring you to Venice Beach in beautiful Southern California and you sit in the house all day driiinking!"

So to appease El Presidente of the Better Youth we walked along Venice Beach to witness the most incredible freak show on Earth. There were rollerbladers with wind sails, pensioners on sand bikes with foot-wide tyres, an army of Lycra-clad joggers with Walkmans, musclemen, hippies, sword swallowers, fire eaters, pinheads, and absolutely no overweight people whatsoever.

We laughed harder than what was probably necessary for far too long at other people's expense and just where the footpath curves at the end of Venice Beach and heads towards Santa Monica, Hairy dropped his trousers for some reason and ran along the sea front with them around his ankles. The rest of us ran across the sand until we fell over laughing before heading back to Shawn's and then he took us to a bowling alley in Santa Monica for the 'Great Southern Californian Punk Record Label Bowling League'.

At the bowling alley the brothers Stern tried to get us to bowl but we politely declined on account of being stupid British people with absolutely no idea of the idiosyncrasies of American culture. We opted instead to play pool and of course drink beer before witnessing the macho competitiveness of amateur bowling Americans.

Soon bored of pool we ended up waiting around outside the bowling alley to avoid the punk rock schmoozing, the final outcome being B.Y.O. beat Epitaph Records in a play-off with Fearless Records and Hopeless Records trailing. We had no idea what any of this meant but we figured it had to be a good thing as we were clearly on Team B.Y.O.

After they'd concluded proceedings, and before Shawn and Mark parted ways for the night, we all stood outside the bowling alley illuminated by the humming street lights and listened to the Sterns tell us how they'd started this little bowling league after André at the label had heard Fat Wreck Chords had done something similar in San Francisco. As a result they'd been thinking about starting a punk rock bowling festival in Las Vegas, as they liked to spend time gambling and drinking there on holiday weekends. They held their first tournament and festival the following year in 1999. Punk Rock Bowling? It'll never catch on.

CHAPTER 36: YOU'LL HAVE TO BE MORE PACIFIC

I woke up numerously during the early hours of Tuesday June the 23rd in jet lagged confusion and at one point Hairy shook me awake saying I'd been moaning in my sleep. I quickly realised that I'd somehow wedged my head into the corner of the old sofa, had an episode of sleep paralysis and had been watching myself sleeping from the ceiling. After the fear and cold sweat subsided I eventually fell back to sleep putting it all down to disruption of the Circadian rhythm.

After everyone got up in the morning we walked a couple of miles along Venice Beach to an empty Muscle Beach and then arrived at Santa Monica pier. Near the pier there were some gift shops and food places and one was selling a variety of hot dogs. With a confused look on his face Will turned to me and asked, "What's a polish dog?" (as in furniture polish) and everyone fell about laughing as I explained to him that it was referring to the nationality of the hot dogs on offer not that they were made out of polish.

After we'd regained our composure we walked along the pier before heading to the Third Street Promenade where we all ate Cajun veggie food, I bought Peter Pan figures for my son, Jon bought a Welsh flag, Will bought cigarettes, Hairy bought gigantic trousers, and Graham bought nothing to protest the injustice of the Capitalist system.

We got back to Shawn's and it was quiet with no-one home, so we headed back down the lane to Venice sea front and of course ended up at a bar with pitchers of beer. Later in the evening we ended up in another bar on the beach and Will was served a beef samosa by mistake after ordering a veggie one, got angry after biting into it, and left with Graham and I after refusing to pay for it. Hairy and Jon quickly followed suit and our systems shut down laid out on whatever we could find in the half empty apartment.

CHAPTER 37: HALF AS MANY MEXICAN GUYS

In the morning of Wednesday the 24th of June Will, Graham
and myself went to the B.Y.O. office and I typed up a mail
interview for a zine before talking with Mark and Shawn
about the intricacies of the upcoming tour. We'd left
Hairy and Jon to wander Venice and they later told us that
they'd wiled away the day trying to photobomb the filming of
Baywatch, Hairy trouserless of course. Hopefully they're
immortalised lurking in the background of an episode of
season nine.

Mark Stern took the rest of us to the screen printers in a
workshop at the rear of a house on a hill somewhere where
a team of Latino guys were busy finishing off our FOUR
LETTER WORD tour merchandise. As we left, Mark reversed the
van into an expensive chair outside next door's business
unit and we sped off back to Venice to meet up with the
others, then headed back out with Shawn to Guitar Centre
in Hollywood to pick up some guitar strings, plectrums
and drum breakables courtesy of the gold plated B.Y.O.
account. The others got what they needed while I wandered
around trying to look like a musician and failed.

Later as evening approached Shawn took us to a plant hire
place to rent some large wheelbarrows as our real intended
use as free imported labour came to light. I had to loan
Shawn the cash for a huge walk-in skip/dumpster and we were
taken back to his place where we were ordered to set about
shifting the forty or so tons of broken concrete piled
up in his yard that had been left as a result of all the
building work he'd just had done. We set about loading the
wheelbarrows by hand and wheeling them out onto the busy
Pacific Avenue to dump their contents into this large open
ended steel receptacle as cars whizzed by.

Our makeshift abode was dubbed 'Shawn Stern Concentration
Camp' from this point on and about ninety minutes after we
finished the task, sweating and exhausted with bleeding hands

under the buzzing street lights of Pacific Avenue, Shawn came out to inspect our work and declared his satisfaction with a job well done, "Maaan, that would've taken half as many Mexican guys a quarter of the time".

As payment for this grisly ordeal he then bought us a tofu Thai meal at a local restaurant that cost a fraction of what half as many Mexicans would've charged him for the job we'd just done, and the five us looked on open-mouthed and drooling as he served himself our pay onto his platter with a large ladle while we sat like Victorian street urchins, scraping out any remaining morsels and sharing them amongst ourselves.

I'm joking of course, we chatted and laughed while wolfing Thai curry and downed a few beers before heading back to Shawn Stern Concentration Camp for some much needed shut-eye, taking it in turns to stretch out on the old sofa.

On Thursday the 25th of June Graham and Hairy left early to hire a car for our trip to our American debut performance in Phoenix, Arizona. I was looking forward to it as I'd never been to Phoenix, they returned in a plush new car and we left for the freeway at about 9:30am.

This was Graham's first time driving on the American roads and his first experience of their grid system and special talent for hiding freeway entrances. So after getting lost for an hour we finally found the highway to hell and drove east out of Los Angeles past the huge San Gorgonio Pass wind farm near Palm Springs in West Coachella valley, and then onwards out into the barren and inhospitable Sonoran desert until at last at around 5pm we reached Phoenix.

We drove around for what seemed like an age trying to find the venue at 2949 West Osborn Road out on the north west edge of Phoenix, then finally we hit upon this flat roofed, single storey, fenced-off building at the end of a deserted industrial estate and I spotted 'The Vortex' sprayed by stencil on the door in small letters. We'd found it.

Accustomed to the cool sea breeze of the Californian coast we weren't prepared for the climate of Arizona as we pulled up and exited the comfortable air conditioned car, stepping out into an atmosphere not unlike the surface of Venus. Four agonising hours later we'd managed to walk the fifteen or so yards to the venue and we knocked on the door panting and parched.

Inside wasn't much different and we found ourselves in a pitch black and trashed warehouse squat with bodies in various rooms among the catacombs. We stumbled across a body that moved and it was a hippie gentleman who kindly turned some lights on presenting us with the stage, a concrete floor fronted by a seven foot high chain-link fence topped off with some fetching barbed wire.

Was this to protect the audience or the band? The hippie guy then pointed out the ten foot wide red circle painted in front of the stage, "This is the pit", he exclaimed, "We painted it red so you can't see the blood." Gulp! What the fuck was this, punk rock Blues Brothers?

As we struggled for breath in this parched incinerator environment, a white van pulled up and out popped our label mates JON COUGAR CONCENTRATION CAMP, namely Chris Fields, Dave Swain, Rory Rogers and their merch guy, only known as Junior. Swift introductions were accompanied by handshakes and we found ourselves on a wrecked sofa parked against a fence opposite the back door drinking beer. Soon enough we were talking like we'd known each other for years as we watched some ants weave their way through the cracks in the earth, and the heat suddenly seemed bearable.

JON COUGAR CONCENTRATION CAMP all wore jeans with turn ups, white t-shirts and black leather jackets. They looked like they were ready to rumble and we later found out that their stage show backed this up. Chris Fields was the vocalist and guitarist, a wry character, unshaven with greasy hair that would repeatedly fall over his face before being swept back. Dave Swain on the bass had a twinkle in his eye that had acquired a few drinks in their time. Rory Rogers from B.Y.O. was standing in on the drums, the third of this trio who all looked like quintessential clean-cut American kids. Their pal Junior was also a friendly guy and it seemed cool that we were due to play some gigs together.

Then we met the promoter, a weasely man who got his excuses in early by complaining about the fact that ALL were playing down the road in Tempe that night. Then we were confronted by the club owner, a flat-topped, tattooed, muscle-bound goon who looked like an ex-Marine and prattled on and on about how he usually made a fortune promoting raves. Soon after, an ex-MANDINGO drunk guy came up for a chat before we realised that it was getting late and only about twenty people had turned up.

Some of the locals seemed a little strange and one particular passing Einstein announced to us, "Around here we knuckle up dude" for no apparent reason. It was about 9:30pm and still about 90 degrees when we were entertained by the stage capers of THREE OUT OF FOUR and THE BEELZE BULLIES before taking the stage ourselves, slightly nervous as we faced twenty desert primates through a fence.

A short, sharp and shit set was quickly executed, aggravated by the pre-1950s vocal P.A. and not even the last chord had died out before the owner started yelling, "Who called my country a ghetto?!" I'd already left the stage thinking everyone else was behind me but I looked back to see the Marine and the Knuckle-Up Dude had jumped on the drum riser and were directing their anger at Will who was packing up his drum gear.

Rory was already on stage setting up his kit and was telling the guy to mellow out when thwack!, Rory copped it twice in the kisser for his obvious intellectual superiority. Complete chaos ensued with sun-baked drunken morons scrabbling to grab all and sundry and each other, in a free-for-all who's-to-blame situation. I looked on in horror knowing full well that I'd introduced our first song with, "This is Rich White Ghetto, this is about where you all live!" My attempt at a smart arse FEAR-style stage banter having more of an immediate effect than I had previously anticipated.

JON COUGAR CONCENTRATION CAMP grabbed their guitars and Chris snarled and taunted the evolutionarily challenged crowd by violently rattling the fence with both hands, the attendant rabble responding in a manner not unlike a pack of stray dogs with a fresh lump of meat thrown in their midst. Three songs later and JON COUGAR CONCENTRATION CAMP just dropped their guitars in a swirl of feedback and disgust and left the building, and we all sat back on the battered sofa outside at dusk in view of the adjacent car park and its rows of pick-up trucks.

At the back of the venue we were fenced in with our vehicles and on the other side of the huge fence we looked on in disbelief as the club owner mounted the back of one of the trucks and proclaimed to the drooling rabble before him, "Don't hit your own, hit the English, fuck the English!" as if he were addressing a blood-hungry mob prior to a lynching. Looking on I asked Jon, "You think it's worth pointing out at this point that we're in fact from Wales?" "Nah mate, I think there's a fair chance that will only inflame the situation further", he quipped back.

Arms aloft, the mob were in agreement with their leader, and as if to display their allegiance a few of the most upstanding circled the car park beyond the fence in their pick-up trucks kicking up dust as they went, waving their fists out of their windows and yahooing, "Fuck the English!" The dust they unsettled blemished the darkening sunset as we gazed in awe at the escalating stupidity before us.

I briefly talked to a few younger members of the audience who were there out of genuine interest in the Bands before we decided to make a run for it. Some of these kids kindly agreed to help us by rolling open the huge chain link gates and 3, 2, 1... both bands floored it and drove through as bemused drunken faces momentarily flashed past our windows as we hurtled on by. As we bumped across the unpaved parking lot to our freedom, liberty and pursuit of happiness we looked back out of the back window to see the pick-up trucks still circling with American flags flying.

We stopped briefly to refuel at a Denny's one exit west on Interstate 10 and laughed about it all in disbelief with our new friends that were JON COUGAR CONCENTRATION CAMP before they headed back to San Diego and we drove the 500 miles back to L.A. overnight. We drove as far as 3am and stopped at the Ehrenberg Rest Area between Quartzsite and Blythe not far from the State line and the spot where D. Boon of THE MINUTEMEN had died nine years earlier and we slept until 5am then drove onwards west as dawn broke.

CHAPTER 39: YOUTH BRIGADE IN THE BOLLOCKS

The road just kept on coming in the early hours of Friday the 26th of June and Graham and I managed to stay awake until he finally gave in and Hairy, the only other driver at the time, took over for the final haul into Los Angeles. We arrived back at Shawn's pad at about 9am and instantly passed out and slept all day until we were rudely awoken by Mr. Stern at four in the afternoon, "Hey, what are you guys doooing? You'd better get up, you've got a show to play".

We got our shit together and headed way out to a club simply called 'Bollocks' at 1702 E. 41st Street on the north east border of South Central and south west of Boyle Heights. The club was run by some pseudo English bloke and everyone was allowed to drink booze in the little alleyway at the back of the club so a few swift ones were consumed among the gutter punks and mohawked leather boys of L.A. punk.

In the middle of the street adjacent to the club were train tracks and before long flashes of lit gun barrels could be seen down the street and a guy brandishing a Taser. As a result most of the crowd decided to quickly retire back inside of the building just in time to watch opening locals TONGUE, a half-male half-female snotty punk band promoting their new album 'Faulty Parts'.

Between sets a couple of us did a zine interview with a guy on the street at the front of the club on his Dictaphone, then we played nervously to a slowly filling club with a few kids seeing fit to run in circles to us as I struggled with my five foot of microphone cord that ran out of a hole that had been drilled in the centre of the wooden stage.

JON COUGAR CONCENTRATION CAMP rocked and rolled to a similar but growing crowd brandishing their brand of incendiary garage punk and blasted through the likes of 'I Wanna See Your Tattoo' and '8 West' before they made a sudden disgusted exit not unlike the Phoenix gig the night before.

After a long pause for equipment changes YOUTH BRIGADE took to the stage and blam!, the fucking place went insane with what seemed like hundreds of kids circle dancing, slamming, diving, pogoing, moshing, the grapple, and whatever else it was called. Many a hit was cranked out by the three Stern originals from their classic 1983 album Sound & Fury; 'What Are You Fighting For?', 'Fight To Unite', 'Men In Blue', and of course 'Sink With California. After waiting fourteen years to see them after first hearing their album and B.Y.O. Records I was in no way disappointed.

Afterwards we drove back to Shawn's place and drank vast amounts of Tecate with Mark and his wife Sandi on the front porch until about 5:30am. Shawn retired after two beers in his usual fashion after impassioned calls for scene unity in his bass baritone operatic drawl. Mark stuck it out and staggered around half-drunk as the sun came up, sharing his punk rock war stories with us like that time he'd been paid for a gig with rolls of pennies and of course the chilli at Calgary Manor. Tears of laughter rolled down our faces and one by one we retired for what was left of the night.

CHAPTER 40: WHISKY A NO NO

After our morning routines on Saturday the 27th of June we called Kris from the label and as promised she picked us up in her 'ol pick-up truck and took Jon, Graham and myself down to Hollywood for a vinyl fix while Hairy and Will stayed at the house to drink beer and sleep.

We hit up Vinyl Fetish, Taang, Bleeker Bob's and one called Stoopid, an upstairs room in an office block corridor on Hollywood Boulevard that resembled a safe room in a private investigators office from an old noir flick. It had loads of security cameras, a wrought iron door, every single punk record ever released, and of course sky high prices from the future on the internet. Unsurprisingly we all left empty handed sneering in disgust.

We dropped Jon off at Guitar Centre as he required more technical assistance for the ailing equipment he was using and the rest of us ate Greek food before heading down Sunset Boulevard past the Viper Room to the legendary Whisky a Go Go. We'd just about managed to load in and the more-rock-star-than-the-rock-stars club employees hit us up with their bargain offer of a live video of our set for a mere $75. We declined then came the great news that they wanted 20% of all merchandise sales. Yeah, whatever.

Soon enough Nick from B.Y.O.'s band THE MISSING 23RD knocked out their brand of melodic Nardcore on the high stage before we headed off to the liquor store for some malt liquor which we drank nervously in the van somehow missing DIVISIA, then it was our turn.

We took to the stage in total darkness and set about setting up our gear. This was it, our big chance, the first time YOUTH BRIGADE and all the B.Y.O. crew would see us play, and at the Whisky a Go Go no less, the stuff of legend. Then suddenly out of the void came a rock'n'roll introduction from a disembodied voice in the gloom...

"Please welcome! All the way from the U.K! FOURRR...
LETTERRR... WORDDD!" The stage lights blazed into life,
the crowd bathed in anticipation, and we were just stood
there like rabbits in the headlights completely out of our
depth. Jon and Hairy were still tuning up and the crowd was
just stood there staring at us in awkward silence.

As you can imagine we played fairly averagely after that
false start to a handful of bemused types who'd clearly
seen it all before. Except of course for the B.Y.O. crew
who graciously tried to fill the huge gap at the front of
the dance floor to make us feel better. Jon's Guitar Center
excursion hadn't paid off as he still sounded diabolical
with Shawn's 'vintage' spare guitar equipment. Two gigs
in with appalling P.A.s and monitors my voice was already
suffering, so I crashed in the van for a while still not
fully over our Phoenix all-night ordeal.

When I came around I headed back inside just as JON COUGAR
CONCENTRATION CAMP proceeded to kick the shit out of
Hollywood, with Chris in no mood for the rock snobs. Just
as I walked in he straddled the stage front and whipped
his cheap guitar back and forth inches above the heads of
the attendant poseurs, snarling as the whole band chanted
the intro, "C'mon, Baby C'mon! C'mon, Baby C'mon!" He
concluded their short belligerent set by smashing his
guitar violently and throwing its remains into the crowd
with Rory joining in from behind the kit. The aloof audience
finally having to move their backsides to avoid the hail of
wood, strings, drumsticks and various guitar parts raining
down on them, launched into their midst by the band.

How do you follow that? You don't. DAMNATION rocked out
with their singer looking like he'd been fired from THE
MISFITS before THE HUMPERS played an average set of leopard
skin rock 'n' roll. Afterwards after avoiding paying the
venue their 20% merch cut, Shawn drove us back to his
place, quietly pondering his decision to sign this band of
complete amateurs from a country he'd never heard of.

151

CHAPTER 41: BEHIND THE ORANGE CURTAIN

We spent the better part of Sunday June the 28th at the
B.Y.O. offices with Jon and Shawn trying to construct a
working guitar cab out of two of Shawn's old broken ones
with kind of average results. At one point Shawn played
with the main fusebox of the office unit when suddenly and
without warning he created arcs of blue lightning with his
bare hands, blowing the power in a couple of the adjoining
units before trying to look unperturbed by his near death
experience. It was just as well he had cropped hair.

I counted out the tour shirts before we hit the road and
had to estimate how many we'd need for a few weeks. L.A. was
bathed in its usual one hundred degree heat as we loaded
up the van with everything we needed for the tour. We then
drove over to Mark's place and marvelled at his pool and
jacuzzi, simultaneously reflecting on the week we'd just
spent in Shawn's building site on makeshift mattresses,
eating from tins and undergoing a regime of hard labour.

After knowing us for a week the Sterns had decided it was
probably for the best to allot us with a driver and road
manager and Rory Rogers pulled the short straw from the
B.Y.O. staff, fresh from his tour drumming for JON COUGAR
CONCENTRATION CAMP. Apparently he didn't mind as he wanted
to stay on the road due to a recent relationship break up.
We thought he was just saying that, but one person's misery
can be another's good fortune, and Graham breathed a sigh
of relief as he was off the driving hook for now.

We drove out to Anaheim in Orange County and a club called
'Public Storage' at 1652 Lincoln Avenue, arriving at about
6pm as DAMNATION were playing their punk rock to a crowd
of twelve year olds. Then a blonde guy in shades walked up
in the parking lot and said, "Hey, how ya doin'?" I looked
at him bemused, reached out and lifted his sunglasses and
it was Bruce who ran Black Bolt Tours, an American I'd met
in the UK who'd driven GOOBER PATROL around on tour for

the last couple of years. He explained that he'd decided to call it a day and moved to California with his wife for a spot of landscape gardening. He enthusiastically helped us load in our gear and even helped us set up. In return we obviously got him on the guest list, a punk rock tradition.

Back inside, queueing with twelve year old punks clutching our drink tickets for sodas, there was no time like the present so we proudly farted across the stage with our usual six song set to an unappreciative bunch of pre-teen rich kids. My voice just about held out and one or two danced, or maybe they were all just rushing to the 'restroom' for wee-wees after all that fizzy pop. We attempted to rile them up with a new song called 'All American War' but the kids just looked on stupefied, and as the last chord subsided one kid shouted, "Next!" That kind of summed it all up really.

After the set Hairy and I visited a local supermarket for some food and I got some Chloraseptic spray for my ailing throat. On our return a few of us were stood around chatting and one of the twelve year old audience members ran up to us and handed us a note. We opened the note and it said, "We are the FOUR LETTER WORDS, we challenge you to the name". We looked up and laughed and asked him what the note was for and the kid pointed at some other kids in the distance leaning against a car smirking at us. We said, "OK, tell them we challenge them to a drinking competition for the name". The kid ran off giggling and that was the last we heard from them as they clearly had no ID.

Years later we were told about a song by a band called THE FOUR LETTER WORDS titled 'Steel Cage Match' with the lines, "We know where we're from, we're not some fucking English scum". As usual no one had bothered to point out that we were actually from Wales but hopefully these days they're old enough to drink, so the challenge stands if they're reading this. It wasn't the last time we'd be challenged for our name, and the next time it wouldn't just be a scribbled note and a stupid song.

JON COUGAR CONCENTRATION CAMP ripped up the stage as usual,
quickly followed by YOUTH BRIGADE who sent the place into a
whirling dervish of pre-pubescent circle dancers reliving
a past they never knew. Adam seemed quite drunk and a
number of newer songs broke down slowly to a standstill.
Even pros make mistakes and Shawn snapped a string and
quickly grabbed the guitar he was loaning Jon and much to
our amusement discovered it was doing the only thing it was
any good at, being out of tune. He gave us a knowing smile
and we threw him wanker gestures in return, laughing.

After the gig jovial farewells and photos were taken with
JON COUGAR CONCENTRATION CAMP before we drove to Garden
Grove and Becca's house. Becca Porter was the Stern's
'sister' and used to work at B.Y.O. She'd been a young
punk rock star in the film 'Another State of Mind' when she
told the world that she wanted to be a clown. The Sterns
reminded her of this when they introduced her to us and she
laughed in embarrassment as if it wasn't the first time.

We sat around like sheepish Welsh people staring at the
posters on her wall which included a giant promo poster for
'Hersham Boys' by Sham 69. B.Y.O. had described our sound
on their promo material for our album as a mix of Sham
69 and New Model Army to which I had scratched my head at
the Sham reference but now it was dawning on me that they
must've been a big influence on the hardcore punks of Los
Angeles early on, so it was a compliment to them.

While the Sterns looked through old photo albums reminiscing,
Becca passed us two four inch thick ring binders explaining
that she had put them together a few years earlier. We
opened them up and we were met with every flyer to every gig
in the L.A. area between 1980 and 1984. We imagined this
stuff at an auction and smelling salts were administered
before we hit a coffee place and then ate Garden veggie
Burgers at a restaurant all sat around one big table before
hitting the sack back at Shawn's. These days the Anaheim
club Public Storage has been renamed 'Chain Reaction'.

CHAPTER 42: YOU JUST SIT THERE AND LOOK LIKE SOMEONE'S DIED

We got up and got clean on Monday the 29th of June and then Rory called and we did one final visit to the B.Y.O. offices and reluctantly handed over our passports (and only form of ID) to Mark as part of the application for our Canadian work permits for our upcoming gigs across Canada.

We hit the I-5 freeway north and through absolute nothingness for six hours, just one long road and nothing either side except for the occasional field sprinkler system. At one point we passed the Harris cattle ranch in the San Joaquin Valley in central California with its 120,000 cows that locals refer to as Cowschwitz, and Will later told us that the sheer vastness of the miles of steaming livestock had made him decide to fully stop eating meat that day.

Five or so hours later we reached Stockton, California, and found 'Chava's Taco House' at 3410 West Hammer Lane, a nice respectable Mexican restaurant amid a suburban corner mall way out on the north west side of town. We tried to find the Stockton Record with the interview I'd done while at the B.Y.O. office but it wasn't in the issue we found.

Soon all the tables and chairs were cleared out of the restaurant and all these kids carried in a nice brand new P.A. System. Everyone seemed enthusiastic and a few punk kids gathered for the evening's entertainment. As usual we bought some beer and drank in the van before heading back inside to watch THE STUPID JERKS do their SCREECHING WEASEL inspired punk before 3AM MECHANIC took the floor, a more mature band with their own distinct sound and style.

We were due to play next and of course the mainly young crowd suddenly had to go home, but to those who stayed we played the best set of the tour to date, possibly as we were out of the perceived pressures of Los Angeles. We went down well and sold a fair amount of stuff, and we even got paid by Ryan the straight-edge promoter.

After the gig, the local kids put all the furniture back in place and turned the room back into a restaurant, then the gracious staff of the establishment fed us some great Mexican food. It didn't get much better than this, no rock club merch tax, no snooty staff, just down to earth friendly owners and D.I.Y. punk kids.

After our feed we were sat around our table talking and laughing when this weird eighteen year old girl, who'd been talking loudly to her friends about how she was Christian and pro-life, butted in to our conversation and blurted out to Jon, "You never say anything do you? You just sit there and look like someone's died." Jon didn't see fit to dignify it with a response adding further hilarity to the already amusing situation.

After loading out all the gear with the clean-cut kids of Stockton we drove back to Ryan the promoter's nice clean suburban family home and had to take our shoes off and sneak in as his parents were asleep in bed and had work in the morning. On our best behaviour, we all settled down quietly to go to sleep and stank out their nice clean living room.

CHAPTER 43: ICED TEAS IN ODD NUMBERS

We had to vacate Ryan's house early on Tuesday June the 30th so we headed off to a café for a fry-up and he found us a copy of that newspaper which we read over coffee. Then we drove really early to nearby San Jose and located the venue 'The Usual' at 400 South First Street, which was opposite 'The Cactus Club' that I'd visited on the last tour in 1994. It was still only lunchtime so we decided to walk around this quiet town full of banks, trams, coffee shops and offices, all modern, leafy and pedestrianised.

We strolled around bored leaving Jon sleeping in the van before driving to a mall out of desperation but it was even more banal. So we bought a cheap frisbee and headed to a park where we ran around trying to look like we could actually do it, failed miserably, gave up and sat in the van listening to a tape I had of Bill Hicks and Denis Leary which wasn't exactly politically correct, so Graham didn't find it funny and left the van grumbling in a huff.

Finally the venue opened and we headed inside the fairly sizeable club to do a soundcheck and were given some drink tickets, and then came the first mistake of the tour. The helpful barman told us that we could have whatever we wanted from the menu, we were clueless, so he recommended some extra tall and super potent Long Island Iced Teas.

Drinks quaffed, a completely sloppy and drunken set featuring four gravitationally challenged grinning buffoons ensued. Will drummed so badly that mid-set Hairy and myself took upon him with mock violence, jokingly beating him around the head and pretending to climb over the drums to finish him off. We were truly, truly awful but what little crowd there was in attendance seemed to enjoy it for some reason and we could make out laughing faces in the gloom. Some of us went into the bar in the foyer after our set and it was packed full of mods listening to vintage U.S. punk. So that's where the rest of the crowd went.

ARMCHAIR MARTIAN were up next and impressed us with their melodic punk before THE ODD NUMBERS did their mod thing with a particularly bad sound to a now full house of modernists who'd come in from making the scene in the foyer. John from ARMCHAIR MARTIAN then gave me the number of where they were staying in San Francisco the next day so we could hopefully meet up and crash there too. Then we met THE ODD NUMBERS, who were very friendly, before I was notified of a situation at the front of the building.

Hairy had been kicked out of the gig for abusive behaviour and according to him a young couple were laughing at him so he shouted abuse at them. According to them the girl had pointed out to her boyfriend that she thought Hairy's especially gigantic shorts were very cool and he should buy some similar gigantic shorts to look cool like Hairy, but by momentarily glancing in Hairy's general direction she had inadvertently invited a hail of paranoid abuse.

I apologised to the couple and headed outside to find the drunken buffoon in the van talking to an equally drunken woman who looked like she'd just been on a heroin bender and beaten around the face with a meat tenderiser. In my usual diplomatic manner I told them in no uncertain terms to, "Get out of the fucking van!" She quickly left leaving me to try to talk to an angry, drunken, rambling Hairy when I wasn't in much better condition myself.

After a while I gave up trying to talk to the Incredible Sulk and fell asleep in the van only to be rudely awoken and herded into a packed school bus in the pitch black outside the owner's house that we were supposedly not to enter. It was hot, claustrophobic, and there was no oxygen. At this point proudly straight edge Graham thought it amusing that everyone was so drunk even though we didn't really want to be from those Long Island Iced Teas, so I threatened him with violence, found my way to the house, threw up in a toilet, and passed out on a couch.

CHAPTER 44: SUMMER OF HAIGHT-ASHBURY

As you can imagine we felt fantastic on Wednesday the 1st
of July, but I pieced together what was left of my brain
and rounded up the assorted idiots. We realised that we
were at the house of some of the friends of THE ODD NUMBERS
and they were very nice people considering the absolute
state of us the previous night.

Then a mad mod with purple hair took us to a Mexican
restaurant for some huge life-saving burritos that we just
about managed to hold down and Jon was so hungover he could
only manage half, staring at it on the plate with dull
lifeless eyes. After this, our van full of hungover ghosts
drove the comparatively short distance to San Francisco
with the straight-edge Rory and Graham up front all smug
in the knowledge that they didn't drink.

Soon enough San Francisco emerged and we parked up in
Haight-Ashbury in the mid afternoon sun and wandered
around aimlessly looking at all the hippie shit on offer.
We visited Amoeba Records and gazed at the vastness of it
all and, bored of being asked for money by professional
hippies by late afternoon, decided to head out to the
Golden Gate Bridge. Soon enough we were driving over it's
monstrous structure, visited the tourist viewing site on
the other side, and took photos of it and each other.

While there, an older French guy asked us in broken English
if he could hitch a lift back over with us. I gestured to
my camera in return and he snapped some photos of us with
the bridge behind. He didn't say a word all the way over,
probably because he didn't really speak the lingo but also
possibly due to the van aroma we'd been cultivating.

We dropped him off and drove down to Fisherman's Wharf
where we walked among the other tourists and looked at tat
shops full of useless trinkets, before taking photos of
ourselves again with Alcatraz and the Bay in the background.

By this time it was starting to get dark so I tried phoning the contact number that John from ARMCHAIR MARTIAN had given me the night before. There was no answer so we wandered around some more before I phoned again, eventually speaking to the guy whose house it was, but alas there was no room at the inn. He said he would try finding us somewhere to stay but when I called back there was no luck with that either. It transpired that our unknown helper was a guy called Joey Cape from a band called LAG WAGON.

It was getting pretty dark and pretty cold as the evening fog began to bite at San Francisco Bay so we decided the best thing to do was to drive downtown again and do something to occupy ourselves, so we hit upon a cinema and begrudgingly parted with $8 each to see the X-Files Movie which turned out to be just a regular extended episode with extra loud special effects.

The film ended and we headed back out into the cold Frisco night to try and find a motel but they were either too expensive or all booked up. Frustrated, we drove right out of San Francisco and found a cheap room at some shithole somewhere on the outskirts of the city because it was better than sleeping on the side of the road.

160

CHAPTER 45: THE UNCOVERED DRAGON SALOON

We checked out early and drove all the way back into San
Francisco on Thursday the 2nd of July before spending an
hour trying to park. We grabbed some food and drove to
Chinatown to walk around for some more tourist action
before driving around a lot more looking for parking and
we ended up in Market Street, a long road with shops full
of beggars, drunks, bums and junkies who all harass you for
cash. A human freakshow of epic proportions it was a bit
like dropping the needle halfway through a RANCID album.

The last straw was an incredibly disabled guy who could
hardly speak or walk following us and begging us for
money. As a result we decided to bail on Market Street and
drove back to Fisherman's Wharf to look at a battleship
and a sub, before eating Subs and heading to the venue,
Stinky's Peepshow at the 'Covered Wagon Saloon' at 917
Folsom St. The outside of this place was the same deal as
Market Street with sketchy looking types and drug dealers
everywhere, and thoroughly fucking depressing.

Soon enough it was soundcheck and beer tickets time. Joey
from LAG WAGON turned up and introduced himself, then my
old friend Greg from SWINGIN' UTTERS turned up too. The
place began to fill up and Spike from SWINGIN' UTTERS and ME
FIRST AND THE GIMME GIMMES was DJing some of the cheesiest
70s and 80s pop music imaginable while an assortment of
large leather clad ladies demeaned themselves by dancing
badly all over the covered pool tables and bar. We knocked
out our crap set pretty well to a largely uninterested
crowd who seemed to be there to drink, make the scene and
show off their hipster vintage threads.

After this I needed a morale booster so I went to the gas
station next door and called home missing ARMCHAIR MARTIAN.
I returned to the fact that unsurprisingly we hadn't sold
any of our stuff and Graham was completely bored sat next
to an equally bored Vinny, ARMCHAIR MARTIAN's merch guy.

We knew nothing about this place in advance and it turned out that the main attraction for the hapless 'punters' at this dive was that there was a little room at the back where late at night there was a 'Peep Show'. We'd thought this was some sort of joke on the flyer but no. Of course Hairy couldn't resist the temptation to soil his underwear and partook of this sordid activity, he even might've wedged a folded dollar or two. No wonder they called him Dirty Hairy, he always got the shit end of the stick.

Eventually, dodging the sidewalk freakshow outside, we managed to load-out and leave, and found ourselves at a house in a quiet part of town with Greg from SWINGIN' UTTERS and his host of female friends. Most of our gang were in party mood, apart from straight edge Graham and my early rising self, and no-one had wanted to carry the backline up flights of stairs, so we opted to sleep in the van in the car park of a supermarket after hearing all the stories of band's vans getting ripped off.

CHAPTER 46: UP IN SMOKE IN BERKELEY

We regained consciousness in the van on Friday the 3rd of July and partook of breakfast at the supermarket's dingy café where I also bought some industrial strength foot spray for everyone, but it didn't really help matters as we were already cultivating what became known as our 'Tour Talons'. After this we went to the house to find an array of hollow men crying like small children after partying all night, while the ladies whose apartment it was came through in fine form and made us all the most magnificent food and coffee. Graham and I explained that we'd eaten and were met with disdain so we knuckled under and forced down a small portion or two, well it would've been rude not to.

Greg then joined us for a trip to the 'Epicenter Zone' record store which didn't open until 3pm so we drank even more coffee, started to twitch uncontrollably, and looked around a thrift store full of multi-coloured Hawaiian shirts and gigantic trousers from 1972 which thankfully managed to stop the constant wailing that came from Hairy's mouth for a few brief moments of peace.

The 'Epicenter Zone' finally opened and Greg waited patiently while Graham and I slammed our vinyl fix. The others sulked in the van at our mild interest in matters punk rock so we made them wait for as long as we could before leaving for Berkeley, dropping Greg off home on the way.

Once over the bay we found 'La Val's pizza' at 1834 Euclid Avenue in leafy Berkeley near the University of California Campus, and the venue was in the basement of the large restaurant. We quickly got bored of our own company and went to a Greek place for Falafel so Graham didn't die of veganism in America and then walked around the legendary campus itself trying to look intelligent and failing as usual. Back at the venue five yards away we acquired our free pitcher of piss beer and then played early at 8:30pm to absolutely no-one apart from some other band members.

After our awkward set, a band called PROBLEM that seemed
to consist of middle aged punk muso types, played next.
Murmurs in the crowd led us to believe that the gothic
female vocalist apparently had no underwear on and had
outrageously flashed her private parts to the crowd. She
then quickly made friends with a large woman in the now
growing audience by calling her a fat pig after she'd been
less than amused at seeing the vocalist's genitalia. You
could've cut the atmosphere with a knife.

Greg Utter and his female friends showed up and next up
was our first encounter with RETOX who were like some
crazed Cheech 'n' Chong themed hardcore band. They threw
huge joints into the audience, smoked 'em, invited people
on stage to smoke 'em and generally acted as a bizarre
soundtrack to PROBLEM almost getting their heads kicked
in by the aforementioned large woman, her boyfriend, and
anyone else who fancied a scrap. Earache My Eye indeed.

Afterwards we helped poor old PROBLEM load their gear into
their van and tried to quell the fast brewing running
battle that was developing in the alleyway at the back
of La Val's Pizza, but nothing was going to stop this
huge violent woman from attacking the goth vocalist, so
to quell the unrest we ended up having a beer in the lane
at the back of the venue, RETOX, PROBLEM, and us, just so
they'd stop getting attacked and abused. We were nice like
that. Eventually the yelling woman gave up and went away,
probably to yell at someone else.

We missed The GOOD 'OL BOYS while all this was going on
and we weren't sure whether OPPRESSED LOGIC played or not
because they were on the flyer but we didn't meet any of
them and didn't see them play. We left soon afterwards in
favour of renting a motel room in Auburn, California, on
our way to Lake Tahoe, with Greg Utter and his two female
friends joining us. They promptly left in a panic upon
viewing the room to buy shampoo and toothbrushes. We slept
on the floor. We were nice like that.

F.L.W. AT SHAWN STERN CONCENTRATION CAMP

THE I-10 TO PHOENIX

GRAHAM (INSET) JON, HAIRY & WILL RESPOND

LOCAL KID TAKES A BREAK FROM THE CIRCLE PIT

CIRCLE F.L.W. PIT (OK, YOUTH BRIGADE)

YOUTH BRIGADE

SOUND AND FURY AT BOLLOCKS

SUNSET BOULEVARD FROM THE BACK OF KRIS' TRUCK

INSET: B.Y.O. OFFICE UNDER MANAGER KRIS

RESCUED END OF ROLL SHOT OF THE WHISKY LINE-UP

theMISSING23rd

AT THE WHISKY A GO GO

HAIRY, DAVE SWAIN (JCCC), WILL AND GRAHAM OUTSIDE BYO HQ

JON AND SHAWN DOING SOME D.I.Y. PUNK ROCK OUTSIDE B.Y.O.

MARK 'BIG DADDY' STERN IN THE NERVE CENTRE OF THE BETTER YOUTH

BYO HQ: HAIRY, GRAHAM, WILL, NICK MENDOZA & RORY ROGERS

B.Y.O. PARKING LOT AND THE YOUTH BRIGADE/F.L.W. TOUR VAN

ADOLESCENT YOUTH BRIGADE PIT IN ANAHEIM

YOUTH BRIGADE

BLOWN AWAY AT PUBLIC STORAGE

FOOD: BECCA, WILL, JON, WELLY, GRAHAM, HAIRY, SANDI, MARK, ADAM, SHAWN

THE STUPID JERKS

IN STOCKTON

3am MECHANIC
AT CHAVA'S

THE LINE-UP AT THE USUAL IN SAN JOSE WITH ARMCHAIR GIMPS

JULY 4TH CHEESE BALLS

TUES THE ODD NUMBERS
4 LETTER WORD
ARMCHAIR GIMPS

THE ODD NUMBERS

JOURNEY TO THE END OF THE EAST BAY

HEADING OVER THE GOLDEN GATE

GOLDEN GATE: OPPOSITE SIDE

AT THE GOLDEN GATE

FOUR LETTER WORD

ESCAPE FROM ALCATRAZ

F.L.W. LIVE AT PIER 39, FISHERMAN'S WHARF

DRIVING THROUGH CHINATOWN, SAN FRANCISCO

WILL BLINDED IN BERKELEY

PROBLEM
AT LA VAL'S PIZZA

RETOX
FREE THE WEED IN BERKELEY

CHAPTER 47: BORN TO SCHMOOZE

The first thing that happened to us on Saturday July the 4th was we got hassled by the arsehole motel owner for some reason before flicking him the V's punk style and driving off upwards into the mountains. We arrived at Boreal Ridge near Lake Tahoe at about 2pm, queued up, and were handed free tickets for something called the Warped Tour, and then found ourselves in a three ring commercial 'punk' circus.

We decided upon entry to stick together but Hairy immediately stormed off as he was overexcited about all the mindless commercial skate punk and I needed the gents on the way in. We missed the only bands we wanted to see, TILT and BOUNCING SOULS, as they'd played at the rock 'n' roll time of 11:30am. So we stood in the sun's searing heat on the side of a mountain watching Civ of CIV punch himself repeatedly in the chest before they got Kevin Seconds up to sing 'Young 'Til I Die' with them. This was quickly followed by NOFX, LESS THAN JAKE, MxPx and other such radio rock drivel, so we wandered about marvelling in disbelief at the attendant corporate stalls like Sony Playstation.

Rory then used the backstage pass of former YOUTH BRIGADE and CADILLAC TRAMPS (and later SOCIAL DISTORTION) guitarist Jonny 'Two Bags' Wickersham to get Jon and myself in back stage to escape the crowd of thousands. He introduced Jon and I to Johnny Two Bags but the others were missing. Rory then introduced us to Chad from ALL and we exchanged pleasantries but when he left Rory seemed annoyed. We were then made to realise that the purpose of the free tickets was for us to intentionally schmooze with punk rock stars to further our musical careers, something which didn't come naturally to four insular British idiots. We were briefly introduced to some more famous punk people but we didn't know what to say so we just stood around witnessing the media circus. Then I bumped into Max from the SWINGIN' UTTERS and we chatted briefly looking forward to our upcoming dates across Canada together.

Next we watched BAD RELIGION through a gap in a tarpaulin at the side of the stage, looking on as a crushed girl got pulled through the crowd and was stretchered off in a neck brace. One by one our other British comrades appeared from the bustling throng on the other side of the fence, we passed the backstage sticker to them and they got in. Then we decided to sit way-off backstage on a digger and looked on as various bands like THE SPECIALS and RANCID walked past with their guitars on their way to the stage.

Up next were our best buddies from London STRUNG OUT and we looked on in awe as the singer did a ten minute football style warm-up followed by screaming and posing and pulling punk faces at a black curtain at the back of the stage complete with an air microphone, thinking no one was watching him. As it turned out the warm-up was more entertaining than the set. Then it was RANCID's turn to take the main stage with a crowd response not unlike a BEATLES concert. They were introduced by one of THE SPECIALS who proclaimed, "This is the future of rock'n'roll!" and after it all ended THE ODD NUMBERS, who had just driven all night and day to get here, played the closing slot. Imagine playing a vast open air gig and watching 6,000 people exit during your first song leaving nothing but a trail of trash and dust in their wake. Well that's what happened.

We briefly chatted with the guy on the BOUNCING SOULS stall about our fellow B.Y.O. status and he gave us some patches and stickers before we walked through the largely empty mile long car park to our van as various proud citizens let off fireworks to express their independence from us British losers. By now it was 9pm and Greg and his female pals had long gone so we drove the hour back to Auburn where we had been the night before and found a Mexican restaurant in Truckee on the way, and then Will asked us to check his sore throat. We were met with the sight of what looked like strawberries so we popped into a local hospital where he was served up some antibiotics and a bill before finding a nice cheap motel room to sleep.

CHAPTER 48: I'VE MET SOME FOUL-MOUTHED PEOPLE IN MY TIME

We drove back towards Lake Tahoe on Sunday the 5th of July taking in some amazing Alpine-style scenery and marvelled at the huge lake. As we drove around the circumference of the lake trying to find the venue we realised we had no idea where it actually was so we pulled off the road in a heavily wooded area and discovered an older lady sweeping her yard, so we asked her for directions.

Graham leaned out and asked from the window and she happily supplied us with directions to the bar somewhere on the edge of town. Then as we were pulling away she waved us to stop and asked about the Welsh flag that Jon had draped across the back window. Graham explained that he was English but we were a band from Wales and she told us in amazement that she was also originally from our hometown of Cardiff. It wasn't the first time that this had happened.

Soon enough we were wandering around the centre of South Lake Tahoe, walked through a couple of huge and surreal casinos, and then found great adolescent amusement at stepping back and forth across the State line that separated California and Nevada right down the middle of the street.

Eventually we headed back out of town to 'RoJo's Tavern' at 3091 Harrison Avenue and hung around outside in the van drinking coffee, and later some beer. Some local morons turned up outside for a while and tried to intimidate us with their talk of coming down to the gig later to bash some skulls, thankfully it was all talk.

John the total loon from RETOX and the GOOD 'OL BOYS, which was practically the same band swapped around, made an appearance and entertained us with his half-crazed and sexually perverse conversations only to later state without irony, "I've met some foul-mouthed people in my time, but you guys are the most foul-mouthed fuckers I've ever fucking met!"

The gig that night was in the basement below the bar of the establishment, as usual, so we traversed the stairwell at the back with our amps and got a round in. Hairy of course had his usual two small American beer-coloured glasses of froth and suddenly switched from Dr. Heckle to Mr Snide.

We watched RETOX and then THE GOOD 'OL BOYS rip through insane sets including "The Devil Went Down to Georgia" and their various songs about drugs and bestiality, telling the bemused crowd at one point, "We're the founders of the 4H Club: Hens, Hogs, Horses and Heffers". They finished up with the sex obsessed singer John insisting on a wet t-shirt contest to conclude the set but with no willing female participants forthcoming he mainly managed to only soak himself on his own in front of the stage.

We set up and somehow managed to play something closely resembling music to the inhabitants of this strange snowboard resort in high summer, and they seemed to get into it and bought a couple of things so we spent some time afterwards talking to people from the small crowd.

Outside afterwards John from RETOX demanded a signed copy of our tour 7" 'Do You Feel Lucky, Punk?' as we were climbing into the van, something we weren't accustomed to, so after much umming and aahing I silently hatched a plan. I signed Jon's name and passed it to him with a wink, he smirked and signed Hairy's name, and so on, and we all signed each other's names on our 7" and John RETOX was none the wiser. That was the only record we ever signed, except we didn't. Why ruin the artwork? I'd spent ages on that.

It transpired that the RETOX bass player's dad had recently passed away and the bassist had inherited a ton of money and as a result had booked two rooms in Harrah's, a huge posh casino hotel in South Lake Tahoe for the night. The downside was they had the beds and we got about three hours sleep on the floor of a plush room on the fiftieth floor with a TV in the bathroom. But at least it wasn't the van.

CHAPTER 49: HUMBOLDT FROM THE BLUE

On Monday the 6th of July we parted company with the Berkeley nutcases known as RETOX just as they were coming around in the hotel and we left Lake Tahoe at 9:30am as we knew we had some distance to cover that day. Then we drove, drove and drove all day for seven hours taking in some more amazing scenery in the mountains at 110 degrees; lakes, trees, lakes, and a few hundred thousand more trees.

Gradually we descended through even more mountains in blazing heat and then as we turned a corner and the sky was suddenly grey, clouds covered the peaks, it was misty, freezing cold, and looked and felt a lot like the green green grass of home. As Jon wiped a homesick Welsh tear from his eye we realised we were in Humboldt County in Northern California, with a climate not unlike Fishguard.

We drove through the mist to the 'Six Rivers Brewery' at 1300 Central Avenue in McKinleyville and fell into this big restaurant full of teenage kids. Inside there was already a young band called JOYSTICK playing, yeah you guessed it, SCREECHING WEASEL type pop punk. It was the late Nineties after all. We were informed of a free food allocation so we ordered our meal of veggie burgers but then immediately had to put them on hold when we were told that we were playing immediately at 7:30pm, and we were the headliners.

We still hadn't got our passports back from Mark from the label and Canadian immigration so we couldn't drink, at a fucking brewery. So after composing ourselves we announced that we were straight edge for one night only and we were going to attempt to somehow play sober. This was alien enough for us as it was but to top it all off the whole thing was being filmed for a local cable TV channel so of course Hairy dropped his trousers to make sure the camera was trained on him. All the kids seemed to love it though, our set, not his lack of pants, so being sober in a cold nervous sweat wasn't that bad after all.

After the set we ate our cold hard veggie burgers sat on little plastic chairs and then packed up and left at about 9:30pm, but not before being approached by a few old fellas outside. They'd turned up to the gig as they'd read an article about us and the gig in a local Humboldt newspaper that bore the legend, "There's More From Wales Than Tom Jones". Well aye butt, but not much.

It turned out that these friendly old blokes all claimed Welsh heritage and had come to see a Welsh band. Maybe their ancestors had once made that same trip we just had and as they'd turned that corner around the hillside and were met with the Welsh style mists of McKinleyville they'd decided to stay, who knows? Anyway, after we told them we were all related to Tom Jones they bought everything we had on offer and waved us off, waving our t-shirts at us like they'd known us all our lives. Well it's not unusual.

The band coffers suitably lined we drove the twelve miles south across Arcata Bay to Eureka, Jon and I grabbing a couple of beers at a local store before we arrived at the 18-year-old promoter Monica Topping's family home on K Street where we cracked open a few cold ones and laid out on the living room floor while her family slept upstairs. We had to be quiet so of course being serious punk rockers there was the odd mumble and a few giggles followed by outbursts of laughter before finally we shut the fuck up.

CHAPTER 50: DROP AND GIVE ME TWENTY

After the first decent sleep in a fair old while on Tuesday
July the 7th our host Monica let us do our laundry, her
mother politely declining payment. Her generous family let
us use the phone, the internet for the first time, and even
fax an incredibly disgusting cartoon of ourselves to B.Y.O.
before we headed out to a local park and walked amongst the
Redwood trees where Monica told us they'd filmed the forest
scenes of Endor in Return of the Jedi.

Back out of the woods we chucked the frisbee at each other
for a while in a park, went on the swings, and generally
acted like a bunch of ten-year-olds. Then after eating a
pile of Subways for lunch Graham pointed out that the van
was shaking pretty badly and it wasn't down to our recent
weight gain, so we pulled into a local garage to discover
that one of the back tyres was shot and the mechanic fitted
a new one for $65.

Van fixed, we headed back to the Topping house to discover
that Monica's nice biker parents had left us even more
food, so we ate that and sat around stuffed until about
9pm before heading off to a local bar, the 'Vista Del Mar'
at 91 Commercial Street down by the Eureka Channel, which
was only five minutes away next to some commercial fishing
companies. Then for some reason we decided to play for free
unannounced, as if that mattered.

While we were outside Monica's family pulled up on their
motorbikes and feeling indebted I gave her little sisters
a couple of the 'girlie shirts' B.Y.O. had made us for the
tour. Yes 'girlie shirts', well it was the late Nineties
after all. This made their day and apparently her sisters
still remembered us years later because of it.

We waited for the real band LONGFELLOW to turn up and
then we jumped up and did our usual short and shit set.
We started off with a death metal intro, which disturbed

the local pop punk kids, before our usual 'melodilicious' (an actual single word review of our album) drivel. Rory the driver jumped up and played bass on 'Chemical Sunrise' while Hairy practised his dance moves in his long flowing gigantic trousers. Rory got up again to do backing vocals on our cover of 'Six Pack' and in the throes of BLACK FLAG appreciation Graham dropped and did twenty press-ups on the stage in front of us for reasons only known to him.

Afterwards we got slowly but surely drunk while LONGFELLOW played a solid set, squeezing in covers of 'Pizza Tran' by the VANDALS and 'The Crowd' by OPERATION IVY. Afterwards it turned out that they were a really friendly and enthusiastic band so of course we end up getting completely wasted with them. Jon downed Tequila in a manner akin to a hardened alcoholic, quietly wincing as his groaning liver shivered, and we briefly visited LONGFELLOW's mobile home that they toured in before heading back to Monica's stupidly late under the marine layer of Humboldt County fog, slowly falling unconscious scattered around the ground floor of her family home for a second night.

CHAPTER 51: NOW YOU'VE PUT YOUR BIGFOOT IN IT

We woke up really sick and hungover on Wednesday the 8th of July, especially Jon, partly due to the fact that it was 6:30am and we had an all-day drive to Oregon. We said goodbye to the Topping family and drove north following the coast up the 101, most of us managing to hold down a meagre breakfast, feeling like we had tarmac lining our mouths and eyelids, at a Portakabin masquerading as a truckers café amongst the mists and Redwood forest slap in the middle of Sasquatch country.

Inside the Portakabin there was a big map on the wall next to us of the local area with all these coloured pins stuck all over it. So after mumbling between ourselves over our scrambled eggs and breakfast potatoes we asked the woman who ran the place what the pins were for. She looked up, fixed her one eye on us, waved her oily spatula and said, "Why that's all them there Bigfoot sightings 'round 'ere".

Plastic chairs squeaked on cheap vinyl flooring as we hurried out of the truckers café, clambered into the van, and got the hell out of there. We didn't look back, driving all day again, passing out, feeling sick, and drinking water, until finally the hangovers retreated.

We left California and entered Oregon, driving what seemed like a few hundred more miles uphill passing the Three Sisters volcanic peaks, stopping briefly to take photos of the vast 'Sea Of Lava' flows, and finally we reached the top of the plateau and drove into Bend in the early evening to apparently play a party.

We met up with Mark the local punk promoter and set our gear up on the grass next to the tree-lined Deschutes River while kids floated by on tyres. The whole thing was executed in no time all laid out on a tarpaulin. Mark left us to go and pick up supplies and within ten minutes boredom set in so I sat at the drums and a quiet, out of time, badly played 'jam' began (I couldn't play drums), but before we could even break into a 'tune' two police officers appeared and everyone fell into silence looking at their shoes.

Politely but firmly the cops explained that we couldn't play outdoors and we weren't about to argue as we'd still not got our passports back from B.Y.O., our only form of Identification. Mark the promoter had previously cleared it with the local constabulary but for some reason these cops were unaware. Mark returned a while later to hear the news and was somewhat annoyed so he called the cops a few times and they said they'd return but they never did.

Meanwhile a large amount of people had gathered for the party telling us repeatedly, "Fuck it, do it anyway!" But seeing as we'd probably get deported if we were arrested we opted out. Feeling less than punk we packed up and hung around for a while before driving to a local Denny's to eat and then to another address we'd been given to stay for the night. We found the house and it looked like the entire, largely teenage, riverside party had moved there while we'd been trying to find it. I slept in the van.

193

CHAPTER 52: GOING SLOWLY AROUND THE BEND, OREGON

As usual I woke up early on Thursday the 9th of July being
slowly pressure-cooked in the fragrant tour van. After I'd
run the van for a while to use the air conditioning to cool
back off I wandered around Bend on my own and drank coffee
I bought at a local café while waiting for the others to
wake up.

Another problem with the van had come to light, the brakes
only worked intermittently and Graham said it sometimes
felt like he was pumping a foot pump and seeing as we had
a lot of driving down steep mountains on the other side of
Bend, we took the van to a small local garage.

The guys who ran the place were pretty friendly, one of
them telling us he was born in England, and they filled us
in on what to expect at the Canadian border. They charged
us $150 to replace the brake pads and we left the van with
them to go and to eat pizza and look at records before
ending up in the garden of the house we'd crashed at to
discover it had a pool and a trampoline.

After trampolining like idiots we sampled America's ultimate
indoor competitor sport of bowling at the nearby Bend Lava
Lanes. Most of us had never done it before but we didn't do
too badly, getting over 100 points each, except for Graham
who seemed to think the point of the game was to throw the
ball up into the air and down the gutter at the side.

We picked up the now repaired van at 5:30pm and went back
to the house where we'd stayed. I crashed out, Jon drank a
40 ounce, Graham wrote a letter, and for some reason Will
and Hairy showed off to teenage girls over ping pong. Then
finally we got our passports back from Mark at B.Y.O. via
Mark in Bend and breathed a sigh of relief.

After a short evening drive we arrived at the 'Evil Sister
Saloon' at 17 North West Greenwood Avenue next to a freeway

underpass at about 9pm. We unloaded, set-up and drank a
hurried beverage before playing to a meagre, broken looking
crowd of locals, all looking sideways at us down a long
bar. The sound was bad and we couldn't get into it in this
uninviting room, then to make matters worse Jon snapped a
string mid-song, but then somehow managed to re-string it
and tune it up in record breaking time, continuing to play
the same song before it had finished. Of course during the
next song it went out of tune again as the string was new
but I was still impressed at his guitar tech wizardry.

As I was yelling into the microphone trying keep my shit
together I noticed Hairy acting oddly next to me on stage,
pulling faces. This continued for the remaining two songs
which by now I wanted over with and forgotten about. We
finished the set and jumped down from the high stage to
a silent bar and no sooner had we done this than Hairy
started shouting at Jon right in front of the stage. Jon
looked confused and Hairy's face contorted angrily and he
threw half a pint of beer straight in Jon's face at point
blank range offering him outside for a fight. All the while,
the still silent patrons carried on staring at us sideways
down the long bar.

I quickly grabbed Jon and took him outside to the yard
at the back of the bar where he paced around turning the
air blue saying that he had to stop himself from reacting
because the tour was more important than one snapped
string. He gradually calmed down and we tried to work out
Hairy's worsening behaviour before going back inside and
not another word was said on the subject, or anything much
at all afterwards, and not even an apology from Hairy.

Back inside I briefly talked to a guy called Dylan in the
bar after our set who told me he was Welsh and we left
Bend as soon as possible at 10:30pm with our tails between
our legs and drove all night north to Seattle with Mark
the promoter from Bend hitching a lift with us to act in a
friend's film in Seattle.

CHAPTER 53: DISORDER AT THE BORDER

Friday the 10th of July ticked into existence on the van clock as we drove all night through massive forests and past huge mountains through Oregon. We watched lights in the sky travelling at 30 degree angles that suddenly disappeared, we listened to religious bigots ranting on the radio, and we saw a huge shadow in the night sky that turned out to be Mount Hood. Then suddenly Graham broke my half asleep daydream by yanking my tape of classic San Francisco punk out of the player, ranting that it was shit because it wasn't SLAYER, pulled over and went to sleep in a huff in the back. I drank coffee and told poor old Rory my life story in order to keep us both awake as he drove.

The others were still sleeping like babies as we pulled into Seattle at about 5am and parked behind a bar, urinating, stretching and yawning as we gazed up at the Space Needle above us. Half asleep, Jon had decided to aim his stream of piss through the gap in the wooden fence onto a pile of refuse bags. Suddenly the bags started moving and said, "Hey! Whatcha fuckin' doing?" "Oh shit! Sorry mate!" Jon had pissed on a homeless guy bringing an equal measure of disgust and amusement to the early morning proceedings.

We drove to a nearby Denny's for coffee and sat and talked for a while and then Graham asked his new found vegan friend, "Mark, have you got the edge?" triggering hysterics on our part. This question quickly became Graham's motto that we repeated often to people we met along the way, "Have you got the edge?" Mark laughed and went on his way.

In the Denny's car park after our coffee we emptied the van contents out onto the tarmac at 7am looking decidedly sketchy. We'd heard a lot of horror stories about the border and even though we now had work permits for Canada we were paranoid, helped in part by sleep depravation, filter coffee and the insane ramblings of Rory who hadn't slept properly in two weeks, and didn't have a work permit.

196

So we set about organising all the merchandise, rolling the t-shirts inside out and placing them snuggly among our clothes in our bags, before finally driving to the border.

We approached the border at 8am and dropped Rory off around the corner just before we got there as he was going it alone in case he jeopardised our chances. We wished him luck and drove toward the checkpoints in trepidation, where the guards made us empty our pockets, roll up our trouser legs and lightly frisked us before quickly looking over the van. We were then ushered into the main building, perched nervously on plastic chairs, before we were called to the window and handed in our papers. It all went smoothly and within 45 minutes we were free to roam Canada. As we left the office we passed Rory and tried our best to ignore each other before driving away with our fingers crossed.

As planned we headed for our rendezvous point, the first gas station on the right, and waited for Rory. While we waited I phoned our next contact, Jinx Stringer from BRAND NEW UNIT and spoke to his mother. I decided to use the time to shave in the gents while waiting and on my way out I was met by a flustered Hairy breathlessly explaining that Jinx's mother had called the gas station back with a message, our friend hadn't got into Canada. So we had no choice but to leave Rory alone at the U.S./Canadian border.

Later we were told that supposedly Rory had a previous work permit application so the gig promoter in Canada hadn't submitted his name with ours, B.Y.O. assumed his application didn't go through and when he attempted to enter Canada as a tourist and they checked the computer he was refused entry and banned for a year. I looked over at Graham who started to shake, the colour draining from his face, and we thought maybe it was because he'd lost two friends with 'the edge' in one day, but it turned out that it was the realisation that he was now responsible for his originally planned driving duties. Rory later phoned B.Y.O. and they booked him a flight back to Los Angeles.

We left the border and drove the thirty minutes to Jinx
Stringer's house in Delta, B.C. at midday and no sooner
had we met than we all fell asleep in various chairs
until 5pm. We awoke to find his mother had cooked us all
a veggie barbecue which we politely wolfed down, talked
with them all for a while and they took photos of us with
Jinx, during which Mrs. Stringer asked Jon, "So how come
you dress normal and the others don't?" Fits of hysterics
erupted and Jon quietly simmered beneath his calm exterior.

After another twenty minute drive we were at the 'Bridgeview
Hall Community Centre' at 11475 126a Street near the Fraser
River in Surrey, B.C. by 6:30pm. Due to an uptight promoter
and early finish there was only enough time to set-up before
we played not long after doors at 7:30pm. We played OK but
we were still tired and it felt like there was lead in our
shoes, but we tried our best to look enthusiastic.

This was the first gig of our Canadian leg of the tour with
BRAND NEW UNIT, 22 JACKS and SWINGIN' UTTERS, which I'd
managed to blag us on from knowing the SWINGIN' UTTERS
from the 1994 tour with CHAOS U.K. This connection from
B.Y.O. sorting out the dates with the SWINGIN' UTTERS over
the phone gave rise to a split LP with YOUTH BRIGADE a
year later. Bassist Kevin Wickersham had left the Utters
since the CHAOS U.K. tour in 1994 and had been replaced by
Stinky's DJ Spike Slawson of ME FIRST AND THE GIMME GIMMES.

All the bands played well to a very reserved audience in
a cavernous and well lit sports hall, and some holidaying
friends from Cardiff, James Hewitt of ska band SHOOTIN'
GOON, his brother and girlfriend turned up and we talked
to them, which seemed weird on other side of the planet.

At various points in the evening I met and chatted with
Gabe of BRAND NEW UNIT, various passing 22 JACKS and
SWINGIN' UTTERS outside in the parking lot. Afterwards we
drove back to Jinx's, drank more beer and talked politics
until 1am when one by one we fell asleep.

CHAPTER 54: SEE YOU IN THE PIT

Saturday the 11th of July started as a grey and mild summer morning in British Columbia just like back home. We ate breakfast, showered and used the phone before watching Croatia beat the Netherlands in the third place play-off of the World Cup while Jinx helped Jon hire a guitar for $20 for a whole month and finally got us out of the muddy guitar hellhole we'd been in.

After the football we drove through beautiful British Columbia with its Mountains, lakes and waterfalls, they weren't kidding. The downside was we discovered there was no veggie food in any of the service stations in Canada.

Four hours later we reached Kelowna around 7pm and loaded in. It was on the University of B.C. campus at a hall called 'The Pit' with the same tightly wound wannabe industry promoter as the previous night. This made for mild entertainment as we watched him get all hot under the collar about set times and soundchecks in this cavernous hall of glass and steel that was more reminiscent of an airport than a punk club.

Some guy drove Gary, the vocalist of BRAND NEW UNIT and myself to a liquor store and the driver asked if I was German, I replied that I was Welsh and he then proclaimed that he was Welsh too. He definitely needed to work on his accents. We drove straight back and played at 7:30pm, the sound was bad but our set was good to the usual sparse audience. We drank the beer we'd bought sat in the BRAND NEW UNIT van and missed 22 JACKS before catching the end of the SWINGIN' UTTERS set, and after eating burritos we watched the confused trainee P.A. guy struggle at the controls while selling absolutely none of our merch.

After the gig was over we collected our king's ransom of $50 for the gig, spent it on coffee, and began our ten hour slog to Calgary, Alberta. An hour or so later Graham realised that he'd left our CDs at the venue.

CHAPTER 55: FEATHERING THE NEST

We drove through the night until 3am on Sunday July the
12th when we pulled in somewhere at a gas station rest
area and tried to sleep, after hours of listening to people
phoning in reports of local U.F.O. sightings on the radio,
and judging by the state of us at this point we began to
wonder whether they were reporting sightings of our van.

As people tossed and turned and tried to sleep, Hairy ended
up across the front with his head by the steering wheel,
Graham and myself were laid out across the two double seats
behind, while Will took his usual place on the bags in the
back that became known as the Nest. Jon slept on the floor
between the seats and needed assistance to get out in the
morning. During the night I was rudely awoken by the sound
of a shrieking Graham "Shut up Welly!" My snoring had built
to a crescendo not unlike a military jet taking-off. Not
long after we were then all brought gently around at 8am by
Graham's Islamic 'Wailing Allah' alarm clock and somehow
it survived. After I managed to prise my fingernails out of
the van ceiling we walked to the adjacent gas station for
coffee and the call of nature. En route we encountered some
rather bizarre looking Hillbilly people, who looked like
they hadn't encountered civilisation in fifty years, and
they gazed in awe at Ben from BRAND NEW UNIT's blue hair.

All refreshed, we drove all day and encountered the Canadian
Rockies, which were awe inspiring, before grabbing a bite to
eat at a roadside restaurant somewhere that was packed like
a holiday resort, and then suddenly the Rockies disappeared
and we were trundling across the endless Canadian Prairies
that stretched off as far as the eye could see.

We finally reached Calgary at 4:30pm and managed to wash
and shave in what we later found out was the ladies room
at 'The Republik' at 219 17th Avenue South West. It was
still early so we hung around in a corridor and a one Steve
Soto from 22 JACKS (and y'know, ADOLESCENTS) walked up and

introduced himself, "Hi, I'm Steve!" Yeah, we know who you are mate. "I was the one who told the Stern Brothers that they should get you guys over here on tour. I really like your music, it reminds me of all the old bands I grew up on". We picked our jaws up off the floor, presuming he was just being polite, and had a quick chat with him before heading for the bar upstairs to sink a few cold ones before playing at the even more ridiculous than usual hour of 6:15pm. In spite of this a killer on-stage sound enabled a good set, garnering applause, dancing, and record sales.

Needless to say, BRAND NEW UNIT kicked Calgary's arse all around Alberta, concluding with their version of 'It Follows' by MINOR THREAT. 22 JACKS then did their line in melodic punk with their singer Joe Sib doing all those road worn American showman stage antics to try to get the crowd to sing along to songs they'd never heard. The pinnacle of their set though was when our new friend and biggest fan Steve Soto, sang 'Message in a Bottle' by THE POLICE. Afterwards I ended up chatting with them for a while as most of the FOUR LETTER WORD rabble walked off down the street, obviously to a local boozer. Joe, Steve, Bill, Jose and Kelly of 22 JACKS seemed like nice enough chaps.

After a couple of artisan (a.k.a. hand smeared in the van) peanut butter sandwiches I managed to catch the end of the SWINGIN' UTTERS set before Graham and myself found our way to the Ship and Anchor pub where by this time the rest of our crew were complete and utterly shitfaced and I really couldn't be bothered, you know what it's like.

Eventually Graham and I scooped up their remains and shovelled them into the van before we ended up at a guy called Geoff's house watching Dazed and Confused while waiting an hour for some pizza to turn up. By this late hour Graham, who had insisted we order vegan pizza with no cheese to satisfy his religious dietary requirements, had fallen asleep only to grunt negatively when offered any, leaving us with the grisly task of actually eating it.

CHAPTER 56: WE'RE THE FUCKING BAND!

On Monday July the 13th we rose to find Greg of the Utters at the door and we sat around chatting about the differences between Canada and the States before leaving at midday with Greg hitching a lift with the BRAND NEW UNIT boys.

We arrived in Edmonton about three hours later and entered the 'Rebar' at 10551 82nd Avenue. Instantly bored, I left with BRAND NEW UNIT to visit Long and McQuade Instruments down the street before, strangely enough, Ben and I ended up sat outside a pub opposite the venue ordering pitchers of ale and shooting the breeze adjacent to the street in a fenced off area. A local guy called Jody then started talking to us from a nearby table, ended up joining us and buying more beer (these friendly Canadians eh?), and everything ended up completely pear-shaped by about 6:30pm.

We got back to the venue at 7pm and the Gulf War Vet turned road manager for SWINGIN' UTTERS informed me angrily that they'd had to put the stage times back because I was late. We were apparently supposed to play at the rock 'n' roll hour of 7pm, I'd previously been told it was 8pm, now it was going be 8:15pm. In the corporate punk doghouse I hopped on stage and we played well until Hairy snapped a string and spent five minutes trying to replace it, clueless in front of a live audience. I attempted to commentate with my witty repartee, and Jon didn't throw a drink in his face.

BRAND NEW UNIT slammed their way through another strong set and soon after Jon and myself tried to find which bar Ben had disappeared to but failed. Then we heard a rumour that the bands were getting free beer in the bar downstairs so we headed down and Jose from the 22 JACKS kindly handed us a brew each upon entering. We were all having a nice chat when suddenly the evening turned a funny colour.

Joe the 22 JACKS singer marched in and stood between us and Jose with his back to Jon and myself, and I could pick words out words like "We're the fucking band!" and "beer" in an angry tone and Jose's face dropped. Picking up on the weird negative vibe, Jon and I decided to leave.

We found Ben in a bar down the street where he was watching The Exorcist and we tried to figure out what the problem was when Joe came in flustered and apologising saying there'd been a misunderstanding. I confronted him about it as we had no idea what the problem was, but he denied any knowledge of what he was apologising for before leaving.

We headed back to the club and started loading out and he was still apologising and gave us a box of beer. Then we were all invited to the club downstairs for drinks but I talked to Jinx for a while instead, still feeling somewhat strange about the whole situation. We didn't care about beer but it was starting to feel like we weren't really welcome or considered a real band on the tour and it could've been a possible explanation for our set times ten minutes after the doors opened every night.

Word about us being repeatedly late was later mentioned to me on the phone by Mark at B.Y.O. when I made one of my periodical check-ins and it looked like someone had been reporting back or had been complaining about us. The irony being we'd been following BRAND NEW UNIT the whole time on the Canadian leg, so if we were late so were they, and yet no complaints were levied against the Canadians.

After a long while we decided to go downstairs and were all handed beers as we entered by the formerly angry road manager, but we felt out of place by this point among the decidedly drunk SWINGIN' UTTERS and 22 JACKS party so we ended the evening having a laugh about it all before sleeping in the van in the parking lot of a Tim Hortons we'd parked in for the evening a few doors down from the club, while half of BRAND NEW UNIT decided to drive to Saskatoon overnight, the other half staying with us.

Everyone slowly came around in the van on a grey Tuesday the 14th of July and Jon now looked about 63. We grabbed some coffee and Bagels at the Tim Hortons to make a contribution for our free parking for the night and then hit the road with Jinx and Gabe of BRAND NEW UNIT hitching a lift.

Six hours of the vast Canadian Prairies later we arrived in Saskatoon and quickly located 'Louis' Pub' at the Memorial Union Building, 93 Campus Drive in the University of Saskatchewan, a plush pub and large venue with an amazing sound on the University Campus.

Things had changed with the other bands drastically overnight and on arrival we were given a free meal, water, towels, beer, a soundcheck and use of the band room, which made a nice change from mistakenly using the ladies room or truck stop bathrooms with truckers banging on the door.

The place filled up quickly and we played at 8:15pm to loads of interested people in a full club and after our set kids followed me around wanting autographs, which was just weird. Things were looking up and we sold loads of stuff.

BRAND NEW UNIT then ripped through their scorching set as usual, introducing one of their anthems 'Guns For Everyone' with, "This song is about America and it's gun laws, let's hope they finish each other off real fuckin' soon!" I never understood why this band never made it huge with their brand of fast and catchy hardcore but that's the way of the world I guess.

Afterwards we end up in the dressing room while the 22 JACKS played, guzzling beer and cartooning on the blackboard. We watched SWINGIN' UTTERS knock out the hits and they did a good job with their usual active slam pit, watched over this night by gorilla bouncers. We decide to go to the same motel as the other bands and crashed out. A better day.

CHAPTER 58: BROTHERS, WE LIVE IN A WORLD OF SHIT

We grabbed some breakfast in the hotel restaurant with SWINGIN' UTTERS and 22 JACKS on Wednesday the 15th of July and furthered thawed diplomatic relations, paranoia slowly waning. This was a driving day across the vast Canadian Prairies again and over the course of the nine or so hours it took us to get there I collected more and more mosquito bites as they seemed to like the taste of my blood.

We reached Winnipeg, Manitoba, at about 11:00pm, found the hotel where the other bands were staying and BRAND NEW UNIT headed off to a friend's place where they were staying, arranging to come back later to go and grab a beer. We paid for a cheap room in the hotel and watched TV and in what seemed like no time Gabe and Jinx were knocking at the door, but for no apparent reason the rest of the Limeys were all feeling sorry for themselves and didn't want to go out. Not able to raise any enthusiasm out of anyone I said, "Fuck this, I'm off". As I closed the door Hairy fired a snide remark in a whiny voice, "Have fun with your rock star friends". BRAND NEW UNIT rock stars? I had yet to see one of them have a tantrum.

Outside the hotel Gabe said he knew a cheap bar so we headed over there and ordered a round of drinks and talked about the tour so far and the previous night's gig, about which I told Jinx we'd avoided signing autographs and he replied, "Well I guess the British always were a pompous bunch". I don't think he realised I thought it was the opposite, I never got my head around the idea, it made no sense to me, maybe I was wrong, I dunno.

We left the bar and happened upon another place where there was apparently a gig on judging by the noise and it turned out to be the legendary venue the 'Royal Albert Arms Hotel' that had played host to the likes of local B.Y.O. bands the STRETCH MARKS and THE UNWANTED back in the Eighties as well as many out of town touring bands.

Gabe used his power of persuasion to get us in for free and we walked in to some sort of death metal night, there were black curtains everywhere and some turkeys on stage with Satanic make-up introducing their next song with, "My brothers, we live in a world of shit, we are pain!" Before bursting into some dark bludgeoning rubbish.

I leaned over and yelled into Gabe's ear, "What the fuck is this shit?" "It's MORBID ANGEL", he yelled back above the cacophonous din. I checked a nearby poster and they were on tour with a band called INCANTATION and currently illuminated from stage front by green lights, with box fans blowing upwards on their faces, their long hair billowing as they leaned in to grunt into the microphones. The vocalist was somehow still deadly serious with a streak of lightning painted across his face while doing an impression of the Cookie Monster and I couldn't stop laughing.

After three songs watching headbangers with receding hair opt instead to air drum with their index fingers we left bored and headed over to a British-style pub where the SWINGIN' UTTERS and 22 JACKS were drinking. After we'd sunk a couple of Canadian ales I trudged back to the hotel at 2am to find the others all tucked up asleep in bed kindly leaving me the cold hard floor for the audacity of having fun with my rock star friends.

ALL AGES
Sunday July 12
SWINGIN UTTERS
WITH
22 JACKS
ALSO
BRAND NEW UNIT
AND
FOUR LETTER WORD
TIX AT MEGATUNES, SLOTH AND MELODIYA
DOORS AT 5:00, SHOW AT 5:30
REPUBLIK
NIGHTCLUB
219 17TH AVENUE S.W.

CHAPTER 59: DID YOU SEE THAT GUY SPITTING ON ME?

On Thursday July the 16th metalhead Graham was inconsolable after I told him that I'd accidentally seen MORBID ANGEL while he'd sulked with the others in the hotel room. Then we spent the day wandering around Winnipeg where we browsed a decent record shop on Portage Avenue and found a falafel place after seeing only beef jerky and meat sandwiches for two days at service stations across the Prairies of Canada, somehow surviving on water and crisps.

Refuelled, we headed over to the 'West End Cultural Centre' at 586 Ellice Avenue, a large venue with a high roof that looked like an old cinema from the inside and a Norwegian church from the outside. The venue Gestapo set about counting everyone's merch for a demanded percentage and stood there with clipboards manually listing shirts.

Will and I tried to find somewhere that sold beer to no avail and on our return we discovered that the venue sold bottles of Grolsch, for a price. We were leaving Canada that night (maybe that's why the American bands were being nice to us) so we downed a couple of these as a treat, gave Jon the rubber seals to use as strap locks and played at the unheard of time of 7:30pm to the usual handful of people. It was really difficult to get into it when the few who were there were about as responsive as an old folks' home on tranquiliser night.

We did have one sole fan for the night though, he'd jetted in from 1977 and was leaning against the front of the stage with a Union Jack on his leather jacket spitting in my face while we played. After the set I asked the others while they packed up, "Did you see that guy spitting on me?" One of the hyper vigilant stage hands overheard this and asked me if I would like him ejected from the gig. I told him not to worry, left the stage and headed downstairs only to see Mr. 1977 chatting like a fan boy with the SWINGIN' UTTERS in the band room. I smiled to myself and walked on by.

Beneath the stage was a labyrinth of corridors with little band rooms that all had beer in them and as a result we missed BRAND NEW UNIT and ended up talking with Kelly from the 22 JACKS who told us he used to play in FEAR (later GOLDFINGER and these days BUCK CHERRY), Billy had played in FRONTLINE with Joe Sib, as well as EXECUTIONER, and Jose later ended up in THE BREEDERS. BRAND NEW UNIT returned and I took a photo of the scene for posterity.

I talked to the SWINGIN' UTTERS for a while before standing at the back of the stage while they played, stepping up front to take photos. They played well as always and afterwards everyone stood around outside for a while talking while Hairy went AWOL. Graham stiffed the club as usual on the merch percentage front in fine DIY style but the Utters shirt guy Damian wasn't so lucky and the greedy bastards kept him there for ages counting his shirts and taxing him.

So after the whole Canadian tour and each night listening to Spike from the SWINGIN' UTTERS going on about doing Karaoke we finally ended up in a Karaoke Bar which looked like an old restaurant with a chequerboard floor. Spike of course got up for a few croons and this guy could do an impression of any pop star, one minute he was John Bon Jovi, the next Michael Jackson, we now knew how ME FIRST AND THE GIMME GIMMES had come about. We asked him why he had a tattoo of a Heinz Ketchup bottle on his forearm and he replied, "I'm from Pittsburgh man, it's Heinz town".

By this time the others were pretty wasted so Graham and I tried to find food in Winnipeg after midnight but failed and made do with coffee. We headed back to the Karaoke place and said our goodbyes to the SWINGIN' UTTERS and 22 JACKS who were off to play the Warped Tour (originally we'd been pencilled in for a week with the SWINGIN' UTTERS and DROPKICK MURPHYS across the Mid-West after Winnipeg). Then the merch guys' suppressed feelings for each other spilt over into a mock street wrestling match dubbed 'the Clash Of the Tight 'Uns' before yet again, it was time to drive.

CIV AT THE WAPRED TOUR

WARPED TOUR CROWD

FOUR LETTER WORD AT LAKE TAHOE

AT MONICA'S HOUSE, EUREKA
INSET: WITH HER SISTERS IN F.L.W. SHIRTS

SEA OF LAVA & 3 SISTERS, OREGON. L-R: JON, WILL, HAIRY, WELLY

SETTING UP BY THE DESCHUTES RIVER, BEND

BEAUTIFUL BRITISH COLUMBIA

INSET: WITH JINX AT THE STRINGER HOUSE

brand new unit

AT THE PIT IN KELOWNA

AT LOUIS PUB, UNIVERSITY OF SASKATCHEWAN, SASKATOON

GREG IN WINNIPEG

MAX, SPIKE & DARIUS WINNIPEG

BACKSTAGE WINNIPEG: BILL (22J), JINX, BEN, GABE (BNU), KELLY (22J) AND HAIRY

INSET: CLASH OF THE TIGHT 'UNS

SAYING GOODBYE TO THE SWINGIN' UTTERS AND 22 JACKS IN WINNIPEG

JOSE AND STEVE SOTO (22 JACKS), DARIUS AND JOHNNY (UTTERS) IN WINNIPEG

SPIKE DOING KARAOKE IN WINNIPEG

CHAPTER 60: SO WHICH ONE OF YOU IS THE LEADER?

As everyone climbed into the van I tried to explain that we were heading to the border and needed to get back into the U.S. with no work permits, but everyone was so drunk I gave up amid shouting and we pulled in for a final coffee and cleaned out the van before hitting the border in Emerson, Manitoba at about 4am on Friday the 17th of July.

I realised I'd lost my U.S. visa waiver card but thankfully I was able to buy one from one guard while another guard searched our van outside. We were summoned to the counter and while I was filling out forms leaning against the counter looking down and ticking boxes, the officer asked, "So which one of you is the leader?" Silence. I looked up and four index fingers were pointing at my head. Thanks guys.

I was taken into an interview room and interrogated about why I had hundreds of dollars on me (all our pay and merch money, good work band mates) but I blagged it by saying we'd been gigging in Canada on work permits and were heading back to our label in Los Angeles to return the van and gear and weren't playing any gigs in the U.S. en route, and let's face it, it's not like we were making any money.

Free again to roam the U.S. we had to drive right through the night and as usual there were three sleeping beauties in the back while Graham and I sat up front checking regularly in the rear view mirrors to see if a long line of border police cars were in hot pursuit, lights flashing, following us to our next gig at 'Bob's Country Bunker'.

By about 5:30am things were getting dicey as we were running on fumes driving along the North Dakota and Minnesota State line. As the sun came up in the middle of nowhere I kept expecting to see one of those signs that said, "Next gas 500 miles", quietly praying to the punk gods for a service station while pinching Graham to keep him awake when I could hardly stay awake myself.

Thankfully we rolled into a gas station somewhere between Grand Forks and Fargo, complete with tumbleweeds and cow skulls littering the floor, and parked up in the early morning sun. It looked deserted so we decided to rest until it opened, then an overwhelming sense of relief hit Graham and myself when I noticed a light was on and we realised that it was 24 hour. We'd finally found some petrol but as far as the others snoozing in the back were concerned we were running on space dust. Sick of coffee we bought chocolate milk and on we drove with a freshly filled tank.

We pulled over at about 7:00am and managed two hours sleep at a rest area before starting off again and driving for another five hours until at about 2pm we found a one-horse town where a hippie looking café owner kindly let us use his phone. By this point Graham and I were hallucinating so Hairy reluctantly volunteered to do a stint driving with Jon riding shotgun. We reminded them of Jinx's last words the night before, "Avoid central Minneapolis or you'll end up in a traffic jam". And we went to sleep.

We woke up about 4pm in a traffic jam in central Minneapolis (they had one job) with 15 minutes to get to Mankato for the gig and it was an hour away. So Graham took over driving duties again and we got lost for a while before finally reaching Mankato and the ominously sounding 'American Legion Hall' at 222 E. Walnut Street at 6:30 in the evening.

We'd driven solidly from 2am to 6pm and felt like death warmed up so of course what else would we do but locate a local liquor store, and things had gotten so bad we bought 40oz bottles of Malt Liquor and guzzled them down. The gig was downstairs in a brightly lit hall and scores of elderly patriots stared at us as we loaded our gear into the lift. We descended to find about thirty people at the gig below and were told that WHATEVER, who I'd put on in Cardiff with ZOINKS! three weeks before the tour, were supposed to play but had run out of gas and couldn't make it and I imagined them parked up somewhere between Grand Forks and Fargo.

The first band up was MANNER FARM from Vancouver who reminded
us of PROPAGANDHI mixed with BORN AGAINST, the vocalist
had no shoes on and left no doubt about his beliefs with
'Straight Edge' carved into his arm, so Graham didn't have
to ask. They were a good band and nice people.

Next up was KILLSADIE from Minneapolis who we missed due
to beer consumption and got a royal bollocking from Gary
of BRAND NEW UNIT for our slackness and lack of attention
to D.I.Y. Tails between our legs we played our set badly,
mainly because Hairy in his wisdom angrily slapped Will
around the head mid-song, knocking his baseball cap off,
all for the mortal sin of dropping a beat, sending the
general vibe south. Really?!

On our usual negativity trip we'd abdicated the headline
slot to BRAND NEW UNIT and they took the stage, and all
the cash we could've had. For fuck's sake, we were smart
like that. We later pleaded for a 50/50 split but they
just laughed. BRAND NEW UNIT then ripped it up in fine style
before an impromptu set by Chicago's BAXTER, who just
happened to be in town, who knocked out some supercharged
FUGAZIcore to an appreciative crowd. A good gig was had
by all in a fine D.I.Y. style and I picked up a copy of
an AVAIL 10", a MANNER FARM CD and traded the BAXTER 7"
for ours after chatting with the friendly vocalist and
guitarist Tim McIlrath for a while who would soon go on to
form a band called RISE AGAINST.

After the gig we headed off to a young woman's house
where we were due to stay where we were interviewed with
pointless questions about our favourite food and such,
before a few of us tried to sleep on the floor in a box room
full of fairy lights with dolls heads hanging from the
ceiling on string, under a spinning glitter ball, while a
house party was in full swing in the other rooms, at full
volume. A party in every town's punk house gets old after
a month on tour, but to the locals it's the first night,
every night.

CHAPTER 61: DO YOU KNOW WHAT INDIE ROCK IS?

We left the Mankato sweatbox as soon as we woke up on Saturday July the 18th to drive the one hour to Minneapolis and for some reason a stoner band we met at a gas station on the way insisted on swapping CDs with us. In Minneapolis we found the KILLSADIE house where Gary of BRAND NEW UNIT was staying, from the usual address on a tattered piece of paper, and everyone instantly fell in front of the TV.

While some were glazed over at the TV we were told that Extreme Noise Records had moved and was just around the corner at 2524 Nicollet Avenue, so Graham and I left straight away for a vinyl fix followed by Hairy. We picked up some great records, bought phone cards from a corner store and eventually made our way back to the KILLSADIE house to find everyone still sat in front of the television.

Instantly bored of seemingly endless American TV commercials I left to find a phone box and soon stumbled across one outside a liquor store, where I got a good three minutes of talking in before some guy practically drove into the booth and rudely asked how long I would be. I told him ten minutes and he left cursing. Within seconds two gangster looking types approached the call box looking annoyed, one of them banging on the glass in my face indicating in no uncertain terms that I was about to leave the scene. Trust me to pick the local drug dealer phone booth.

I eventually found another phone box and made the long call home I'd hoped for before again returning to the house to find everyone was still watching the goggle box. Finally in late afternoon we left for St. Paul across the river to a downtown coffee shop where BRAND NEW UNIT were due to play in a brick walled back room with some indie rock bands. We grabbed some food from the coffee shop out front beforehand, listened to DAG NASTY on the jukebox and then headed off to a bar with Gabe and Ben of BRAND NEW UNIT and ordered some beers.

We returned to the coffee shop and got in the gig for free joining the twelve strong audience just in time to witness BRAND NEW UNIT yet again scorch the earth with their impossibly tight hardcore, and we finally managed to get them to play 'Do It For You', which had been our introduction to the band on B.Y.O.'s Video Flemloque.

BRAND NEW UNIT had become good friends over the course of our Canadian gigs and consisted of the reserved Gary LaVallee on vocals who came to life on stage, the blond haired Jinx Stringer on guitar who'd mastered our album and had previously been in STRAIN with Eric Thorkellson of FRATRICIDE, Ben Hughes on the bass who'd been in CAT'S GAME (and later moved to Germany) and Gabe Mantle on the drums who later joined the more successful GOB.

The Indie Rock headliner played and as we were stood watching Jinx turned to me mid-set and asked, "Do you know what Indie Rock is?" I looked at him baffled. Afterwards we bid farewell to MANNER FARM who'd also joined us to watch the gig and headed back to the KILLSADIE house, bought some weak American beer on the way and drank until 2am on the porch, looking on in awe as a violent electric storm pounded the pioneer spirit out of the Mid-Western night.

OLD SCHOOL PUNK ROCK LEGENDS
YOUTH BRIGADE

WITH SPECIAL GUESTS:
4 LETTER WORD
PINHEAD CIRCUS

CLUBBER LANG
& THE HEAVYWEIGHTS
HOSPITAL FOOD

JULY 23, 1998 WRAPSODY LIVE
117 N. UNIVERSITY, PROVO 7:00 $7.00

CHAPTER 62: THE DASH TO DENVER

Sunday the 10th of July became known as the Dash to Denver as it was over 900 miles away and we knew it was impossible to reach in a day, so we got up late and ate some breakfast with BRAND NEW UNIT at a café on tree-lined Nicollet Avenue in Minneapolis, before driving convoy style as far as we could towards Colorado. We only managed to make it about halfway before sundown came and went, so we piled into two ageing wood-panelled double rooms at a cheap motel somewhere in Middle-of-Nowhere, Nebraska, and fell asleep to the hum and clatter of old ice machines and the rumble of passing highway trucks on Interstate 80.

We drove for most of the day again on Monday July the 20th and finally rolled into Denver at about 4pm. We parted company with BRAND NEW UNIT who had a gig across town and found our venue, but it looked deserted so we phoned B.Y.O. and they told us it was the right place if it was in a warehouse. We knocked the door again and were met by the promoters Jason and Damien, who lived in the upstairs apartment in front of the small warehouse where they put bands on.

Denver was in the middle of a ten day heatwave and we just about managed to load the gear in without passing out in the non-air conditioned loft before Damien took us out for some barbecued tofu, and we picked up some beer at a liquor store on the way back that had a cop stationed on the door.

On my way out I handed Hairy a brown paper bag that contained my bottled water and the cop insisted on checking it. While Hairy gave him his usual attitude I asked Damien why there was a cop there, "Last year there was a Klan rally here and there was a riot and the liquor store got looted". A Klan rally? What decade were we in again?

We returned to the warehouse to find that the promoters and bands couldn't raise the enthusiasm to play or put on the gig, which was understandable in the brutal heat. So we packed the gear back into the van and headed downtown to the gig at the 15th Avenue Bar on Welton Street where BRAND NEW UNIT were playing, but they weren't there yet so we got the drinks in and waited and eventually they turned up.

THE FAMILY MEN played their NEW BOMB TURKS style racket and then BRAND NEW UNIT stepped up to show us how it was done. During their MINOR THREAT cover we pushed Graham out onto the dancefloor area for a laugh so he could show everyone his 'Have You Got the Edge?' dancing, and he rewarded me with a full force kick to the nuts. Thanks as usual for the sense of humour.

After I'd pushed my eyeballs back into their sockets, SCARED OF CHAKA jumped all over the joint looking like flying mods from Albuquerque. By this point everyone was completely slaughtered and somehow we ended up in Chris from PINHEAD CIRCUS girlfriend Camey's house and crashed out in the studio downstairs.

On Tuesday the 21st of July we arose with major headaches and tried to find which motel BRAND NEW UNIT had stayed at and we eventually found them but Jinx had gone to fix the van's air conditioning. We bought some food and finally he returned and we left, heading north through Fort Collins and then west across Wyoming, passing Rawlins and Evanston, in order to miss the steep inclines of the Rocky Mountains. There seemed to be absolutely nothing in Wyoming.

We reached Provo, Utah, at about 8pm which was a small University town near Salt Lake City in the heart of Mormon country. We met the promoter Lucy Jane and she notified us that there was actually no gig due to a double booking. Deflated, I commented sarcastically, "It's OK, we only drove 550 miles". She took an instant dislike to me. Dejected, we grabbed some of the strongest booze in Utah at 3% and headed to her house where we ended up watching videos until it was time for bed.

CHAPTER 63: IN A RIGHT STATE LIQUOR STORE

We woke up on Wednesday July the 22nd to find BRAND NEW UNIT leaving for their gig with YOUTH BRIGADE in Las Vegas, so we said a temporary farewell as we were due to be playing with them at the end of the tour in Los Angeles. As it turned out we never saw them again. We spent the day pottering around with laundry and phone calls surrounded by Mormons until about 8pm when we headed down to a venue called 'The Café', where we'd been booked to play originally, for a gig. The THE LATCH KEY KIDS played their metallic pop punk before FALLING SICKNESS did their ska-core thing and after the gig we ended up back at Lucy Jane's house with the other bands, where we drank again and crashed out.

We woke up on Thursday the 23rd of July and THE LATCH KEY KIDS had already left, then it was FALLING SICKNESS turn so we traded some stuff with them and said goodbye, they were nice guys. We headed to a supermarket where we bought some cheap food and cooked up a pasta salad so everyone could eat for about a dollar. I popped out to the van for something and found a purse on the driveway so on my return I asked, "Is this anyone's Purse?". It turned out it was one of Lucy Jane's house mates so I handed it over.

Her house mates had previously ignored us the entire time we'd been there, but now suddenly they wanted to talk to us after realising that punk rockers weren't necessarily lowlife criminals eyeing up the contents of their house. So we answered their questions to things such as if we had TV in the U.K., to which we responded by telling them how impressed we were with American electricity and had never seen Star Wars, intentionally pronouncing it wrong. We finished off by telling them that no-one went to church in the U.K. and we all lived off squirrels from the woods.

Utah Valley had one bar and one off-licence called the State Liquor Store where there were no fridges and everything was expensive on dusty shelves, probably to try and put you off buying the demon drink. We found some Grolsch for $3 a pint bottle and Hairy recommended it to some local cowboys and they looked at it, looked at each other, shrugged and grabbed some. We laughed in the van afterwards imagining them waking up the next day in the desert somewhere in nothing but their cowboy boots and magic underpants.

We hit that night's club 'The Wrapsody' (so-called because they sold wraps) at 117 N. University Avenue, and were drinking in a clandestine fashion in the van from Coke cups when YOUTH BRIGADE turned up late with our new tour mates PINHEAD CIRCUS. We'd only just met them but it quickly seemed like we'd known PINHEAD CIRCUS for years. Scooter James was the vocalist and guitarist, a friendly, chatty Mid-Westerner, generally unshaven with a half-asleep bar keeper demeanour. Chris Fogel was also on guitar, dark haired and beady-eyed, he was a budding studio engineer. Trevor aka Trelvis was the bassist, a dusty haired rocker who looked like he'd just left the ranch to come on tour with his tin of chaw. On drums was Otis, a unique character with the disposition of someone who'd dropped too much acid in high school. And finally there was their pal, friendly merch guy Chuck Piekarski who'd come along for the ride.

The bands soon started playing and HOSPITAL FOOD did their skate pop thing before CLUBBER LANG AND THE HEAVYWEIGHTS did skate pop versions of cheesy 80s hits. We played well for a change but three bars into the first song I felt something snap in my leg, leaving me limping. PINHEAD CIRCUS kicked Utah's arse, equalling or probably bettering what we expected of them. YOUTH BRIGADE played with PINHEAD CIRCUS bass man Trevor filling on bass as Adam Stern couldn't tour due to work. They did their usual high quality set and the gig passed thankfully incident free after we'd heard of skinhead stabbings by straight edge gangs at recent Salt Lake City gigs. PINHEAD CIRCUS headed back to Denver to sleep in their own beds for one last time, we visited a Taco Bell and then slept once again at Lucy Jane's house, while YOUTH BRIGADE disappeared to a hotel.

CHAPTER 64: WHAT ARE YOU STANDING THERE FOR?

On Friday the 24th of July we bid fond farewells to Lucy
Jane who'd also warmed to me after I handed in the lost
purse, and I supplied her with FOUR LETTER WORD merch in
return for her hospitality. We left Provo and drove all day
through the rain soaked plains of Wyoming, again to miss
the Rockies. Huge dark rainstorms trailed us all day from
Utah, dragging themselves like lumbering giants across the
dark Colorado badlands either side of us. I fiddled with the
radio and happened upon the BBC World Service channel and
we strained to hear the posh English accents over the high
speed swish of windscreen wipers, like children huddled
around a wireless in the blitz.

We reached Denver about 8pm amid continuing heavy rain
and we got lost as usual in Denver's confusing one way
systems before finally finding 'The Raven' at 2217 Welton
Street. We received a grand soaking carrying the gear in
past the line of punk hungry kids into a strange venue that
you entered behind the stage with leatherette seating and
wood-panelled walls ringing the dance floor like some sort
of big brown diner. At the back was a weird 'bar' which
was a kitchen serving hole from which came pitchers of beer
from an anonymous pair of hands.

We'd been given some drink tickets so we downed our pitchers
of froth passed to us through the hole by the anonymous
pair of hands and missed LATCH KEY KIDS who played for
about 45 minutes while we sat in the van drinking lukewarm
cans as the rain continued to lash down.

Soon enough it was our turn so we hopped, skipped and
jumped through the river running down Welton Street and
clambered onto the high stage. Our set kicked off with
Will's drums flying everywhere because there was nothing on
stage to fix them to the floor and I had to spend the entire
set kicking them back towards him and holding them in place
with my ankle on the narrow six foot deep stage.

Oddly enough the place went off with a huge circle pit of people going mad, to us? We played our usual six songs that Hairy permitted before he left the stage in a flurry of huff and no-one believed we'd finished just as things were getting going, most of all us. We tried to cajole him back on stage but he was having none of it.

PINHEAD CIRCUS and YOUTH BRIGADE kicked up dust in fine fashion, leaving the kids sweating and wanting more, jumping on stage and singing along. We spent some time in the bar before packing up and then headed for the PINHEAD CIRCUS house in Golden, where Chris and Otis lived.

As we parked up outside their place a cop pulled up behind us so everyone walked into the house and ignored him, except for Graham who was locking the van. The cop said, "Don't just ignore me. what do you think I'm standing here for". "I don't know, what are you standing there for?" Graham shot back. The cop then told him there'd been some car theft in the area and to lock our doors, which he'd just done, then the cop left. We slept in the recording studio beneath the house.

CHAPTER 65: WE STANK OUT THEIR BASEMENT

We sat around laughing at This Is Spinal Tap while eating Tacos courtesy of Chris and Camey on Saturday July the 25th, before a comedy show came on TV with the U.S. BOMBS playing. After watching the VANDALS live video the Sterns turned up taking Chris, Will and Hairy to the cinema, while Graham, Jon and myself got lost in Denver before finding Wax Trax at 638 East 13th Avenue for a vinyl hunt.

At about 6pm we headed back to Chris' house but got lost again on the spaghetti freeways in a violent thunderstorm. After getting back we waited for everyone else before driving the hour to Fort Collins, while I slept in the van to try and get my energy levels up. We arrived at 'The Starlight' in Fort Collins at 167 North College Avenue around 8pm and tucked into the free beer laid on by promoter Charlie, whose twin brother Vinnie we'd met in S.F. when he'd been selling shirts for Colorado locals ARMCHAIR MARTIAN.

PISSED CHRISTIANS and SIDESWIPE opened up before we ripped up a breathless set at this high altitude, then PINHEAD CIRCUS went down well but YOUTH BRIGADE didn't after Mark complained over the drum microphone about a drum monitor and left the stage, which wasn't a good look, and you could see on Shawn's face that their 45-minute set felt more like 45 years.

Gig over, Hairy challenged the American bands to a drinking competition in the throes of drunken confidence before PINHEAD CIRCUS headed back to Denver for their last night in their own beds again, YOUTH BRIGADE went to a hotel again, and forgot to pay us again. We visited a supermarket with Vinnie and Charlie before heading to their house where they kindly let us cook frozen pizza and we later sat on their porch as a family of racoons made their way down the pavement in front of us. They gave us a version of the gig flyer they'd painted but we had to leave it as it was too big to carry. We felt bad so we took a photo of it. Great guys, we liked them a lot, so we stank out their basement.

CHAPTER 66: THE SPAGHETTI INCIDENT

We hit the road while everyone was still asleep on Sunday the 25th of July, and I left the brothers Vinnie and Charlie some shirts before we drove through the grey plains of Wyoming again. We grabbed some much needed breakfast at a truck stop near Cheyenne full of denim clad cowboys in Stetson hats, turning to stare at us one by one from various low level booths. The coffees arrived and there was what looked like a large lump of phlegm in mine so I asked for a replacement, we wolfed our food and got the hell out of there, eyes burning in the backs of our heads.

There wasn't a lot to look at in Wyoming, the least populated state, and this was the third time we'd driven across it. I realised that the Little Bighorn battlefield was somewhere along this road and checked the map so we could do something else apart from watch bands and drink weak beer. A while later I asked Graham if we were anywhere near it yet and he said he'd driven past it, to which I got more annoyed than I should have and demanded we turn around. He wasn't happy but doubled back and we visited the site of Custer's last stand, where at this time there was only a monument to the fallen white people. Of course we visited the gift shop where I found a print of the famous painting of the battle by Edgar Samuel Paxson, while Jon bought a copy of Bury My Heart At Wounded Knee, and we left a record of our attendance in the visitor's book.

About ninety minutes later, and nine hours after leaving Fort Collins, we hit the bustling metropolis of Billings, Montana. Surprisingly we got to 'The Shrine Hall' at 1125 Broadwater Avenue on time and discovered that it was a huge venue with a huge kitchen with huge glass fronted fridges full of huge pans of pasta and many crates of beer. We were told it was something to do with the University but later found out that it was owned by the Shriners, so we were expecting a circle pit of kids in Fezzes but it turned out to be more of a college night.

The bands started and THE VETERAN FLASHBAX played their hyperspeed melodic hardcore before another band played that we missed because we were drinking beer, as usual, and being bad punk rockers. We did our set and got a large amount of people dancing in the huge hall, which was nuts and a really good response for a band like us.

After our set we were all in the kitchen and everyone was in good spirits, I was eating a plate of pasta as I'd waited until after we played to avoid mid-set acid reflux, while Hairy was wolfing down his second. PINHEAD CIRCUS drummer Otis climbed into one of the huge stainless steel and glass fronted fridges to cool off and Hairy joined him in the next fridge over. I spotted a stainless steel bowl of fruit salad on the shelf above Hairy's head, so for a laugh I leaned in and tipped it gently, concentrating so that just a slight dribble of fruit juice would land on his head below.

My lack of foresight meant that I hadn't realised that Hairy of course wouldn't find a few drops of fruit juice amusing and instead he took it completely the wrong way, throwing his entire plate of spaghetti all over me covering me from chest to knees in pasta sauce with a scowl. I instantly lost my temper and gave him a light slap to which of course he stormed out of the room crying, telling passing kids he'd been assaulted. This was getting exhausting but was essentially my fault for thinking anything I did would be taken in the manner in which it was intended.

Drama over, PINHEAD CIRCUS and YOUTH BRIGADE played their usual solid sets then we sat around and waited what seemed like hours for everyone to pack up while kids came up to us and thanked us for playing their town, saying hardly any bands ever went to Billings, Montana. The Stern Brothers kindly paid for a hotel room after we'd reminded them they'd been making off with our $50 cut for the previous three nights and Jon, Graham and myself slept while the others partied for most of the night.

CHAPTER 67: I DON'T WANNA GO DOWN TO DEBASEMENT

We checked out on Monday July the 27th and ate some breakfast
with all the bands before following the Stern brothers,
who took us 30 miles in the wrong way, and we bumped across
what seemed like a dusty track eating everyone's dust
through our vents before eventually rejoining Highway 87.

Then we got pulled by the law because some trucker had
apparently radioed the fuzz on his Citizens' Band radio,
"10-4 for a copy Smokey! Some goddamn loser punk rockers
are doing some risky overtakin'". On the side of the road
the cop explained to Graham, "Now Gram (it's how people
pronounced it here) you have to slow down, and if you
CAN'T slow down then I suggest that you get someone else
to drive." Graham got off with a warning, we were lucky.

A couple of hours later and we were in Great Falls, Montana,
and found the venue, 'The Center Stage' at 111 Central
Avenue, and sat at the bar across the street getting food and
of course beer. The venue was like a small but tall cinema
with all the seats pulled to the back. Soon THE RETARDS and
THE RIVER RATS knocked out their punk rock to a handful of
folks and MORAL CRUX were billed to play, but didn't for
some reason. We played well and people got into it.

Outside there was a parking lot running down the side of
the venue and between sets we were sat in the van with
YOUTH BRIGADE drinking beer when a cop car drove past on
the main street to the side of the lot. Quick as a flash
YOUTH BRIGADE grabbed their cans and box of beer and
scurried back inside the venue through the side door while
FOUR LETTER WORD sang in unison laughing, "What we gonna
do about the men in blue? What we gonna do?!"

The rains had followed us from Colorado and as soon as it
started raining all the kids ran inside just in time for
PINHEAD CIRCUS to which Scooter opened the set, "They're
like Gremlins, they got wet and multiplied!" We laughed

and PINHEAD CIRCUS rocked to their usual high standard as did YOUTH BRIGADE, and all in all, the fact that there was hardly anyone there made no difference at all.

After the gig a young woman who only went by the name of E.J. introduced herself and claimed to have once been to our hometown of Cardiff. After the gig we ended up at another young woman's house, who looked exactly like a real life Peppermint Patty from Charlie Brown, with four out of five of the bands in tow, while one band who shall remain nameless, disappeared to yet another hotel.

So it was four bands, all on a mission of alcoholic suicide, I called it quits after failing to stomach the domestic American beer froth and headed for the basement with Chris Pinhead and Graham and we all claimed a mattress and tried to sleep. Then in the dark I could hear rustling and quiet chatter and it sounded like someone else had descended to the basement.

In the gloom I realised that Trevor had also come down the stairs as I could see the light on his camcorder in the pitch black and he was swaying in an inebriated state. Then Chris turned the basement light on and it was revealed that Trev was filming an amorous couple in the throes of passion. Of the two, E.J. got up and left in a huff only to return again after the lights went back out. Almost immediately I could again make out the shadow of a drunken Trevor. This time stood there in total silence for a few minutes in the gloom right above where I was laying, the solitary red light on his camera indicating his presence.

Suddenly from upstairs the loudest retching imaginable echoed through the house as someone started puking over and over again, getting louder with each pan full. Simultaneously Trevor, Chris and I burst out laughing, the lights came back on and E.J. and Graham both left storming upstairs, their basement tryst exposed. The loud drunken bastards upstairs wouldn't let us sleep until 5am and people were dotted around the house trying to sleep.

CHAPTER 68: SO ANYWAY, WE'RE DRUNK BRIGADE

I awoke in the basement on Tuesday the 28th of July to find my hand had swollen up with dozens of tiny spider bites, then we ate some breakfast before following the Sterns again, this time to a bowling alley which was closed, and then another which was also closed, so we gave up and drove in yet more driving rain to Missoula, Montana.

On the way we took the short cut that the Sterns had recommended and the drive to Missoula that usually took two hours took us four. We stopped mid-way and Graham shared his last tin of vegetables with us that we had to prise open with an army knife and share with a plastic lid on the side of the road. What a bunch of punk rock sell outs.

Finally we reached the rain drenched 'Jay's Upstairs' which was a two floor bar at 119 West Main Street in Missoula, with the bands playing, you guessed it, upstairs. We then did an awkward radio interview on tape for KBGA and ate free pasta before returning to the bar to discover that drinks were free all night for all the bands, bad move. By the time we went on at 11pm everyone was well on their way.

Somehow we managed to pull it off in spite of the shit monitors and there being only twenty people in attendance again. Things really heated up when PINHEAD CIRCUS played with the by now incredibly drunk Trevor continually falling into the drum kit and finishing most of the songs lying amongst cymbal stands. This performance was only surpassed by Trevor's usual stint filling in on bass for YOUTH BRIGADE, openly necking shots of Jagermeister between playing the worst drunken bass imaginable and falling over.

A slowly simmering Mark came to the boil mid-set and threw his drumsticks in rage, but old 'Trelvis' just tipped his glass to his band mates with a half-asleep smile and carried on. Shawn saw the funny side and proclaimed in his bass baritone voice, "So anyway, we're Drunk Brigade".

By the time the bands were over at about 1am everyone I saw was cock-eyed and dribbling and staring into a vague middle distance over my shoulder. I got bored of all the drunkenness and crashed in the van for an hour in anticipation of the long drawn out sloppy packing up session I would no doubt play a key role in while everyone fell about later, being one of those lazy vocalists who always makes themselves scarce come lugging time.

I awoke less than amused to find the van full of giggling girls with Hairy and Will in full charisma mode. We slowly packed up and then re-packed up as the drunks got the van Jenga all wrong, then before looking for a hotel Graham backed the van into a post while parking, and he wasn't even drinking, though he may well have been distracted by the fact that E.J. had followed us to Missoula and he was thinking about finding a basement.

We booked a couple of rooms, unfortunately with no basement, as a couple got it on in the bed next to me while I tried to ignore it with my pillow over my head. Jon partied with PINHEAD CIRCUS, YOUTH BRIGADE went to another hotel and Will and Hairy disappeared, no doubt something to do with those giggling girls. As Falling Sickness sang, "Missoula's Gonna Get You!" It well and truly did.

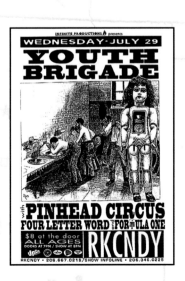

CHAPTER 69: WAS THAT MUSCULAR OR EGO?

Everywhere I went on the morning of Wednesday July the 29th there were hungover bears with sore heads. Will had apparently slept in the van all night and was unsure of Hairy's whereabouts while Jon had accidentally got into the bed next to me with the amorous couple while I was asleep. I left soon after and phoned home for some sanity and then we grabbed some food before beginning our 500 mile road slog to Seattle. On the way everyone slept in the van as usual while Graham and I navigated the uncharted territory behind the PINHEAD CIRCUS van. The Sterns caught up with us at a gas station and Shawn bragged, "I ended the night with two women giving me a massage". To which I quipped, "Was that muscular or ego?" He just looked at me.

After traversing the wet winding forest lined roads of Washington State like a white knuckle log flume ride, we arrived in Seattle in the late afternoon and found the 'RCKCNDY' at 1812 Yale Avenue almost immediately, but not before watching the Sterns change into the wrong lane of the rush hour freeway traffic and disappear.

We unloaded in no time into the big professional rock venue with a five foot high rock star stage and as usual we decided to get a drink somewhere, we walked out of the parking lot and turned the corner and suddenly it looked oddly familiar and I laughed as I realised that we'd accidentally come across the 'Off Ramp' at 109 Eastlake Avenue E, which I'd visited back in 1994, and was now called 'El Corazon'.

We stepped inside, sat down and ordered a few drinks before Mark turned up and proceeded to tell us the fascinating story of B.Y.O.'s big swing band ROYAL CROWN REVUE, their appearance in the 1994 Jim Carrey movie The Mask, how the band later kicked out the co-founding Sterns and eventually stole the band from them and signed to Warner Brothers, and how in spite of all this B.Y.O. continued to receive royalties from the film four years later.

After these light ales and light conversation we headed back to the RCKNDY to see locals FORMULA ONE play to a slowly filling venue. Next up it was our turn and it was hot as we played to the most stuck-up rock snobs we'd come across, even more so than the Whisky. They couldn't even raise their eyelids let alone a round of applause.

PINHEAD CIRCUS received the same response as us and YOUTH BRIGADE received a marginally better one, which was just as well seeing as the crowd had actually paid to see them. The place was full by this point of post-grunge snooty poseurs so we sat in the van, chatted to FORMULA ONE and waited to leave. After the gig we looked for a hotel but PINHEAD CIRCUS booked the last room meaning Graham and myself had to continue searching on foot while Hairy sulked in the van, but we did eventually we find a room. In case you're wondering, these hotels used to cost about $40 and we'd sneak everyone in one room and draw straws for the bed.

We drove down the road to find the PINHEAD CIRCUS hotel early on Thursday July the 30th before we all ate, splitting into two groups depending on who wanted which kind of food. Then we all drove to nearby Tacoma to drop all our merch off at their friend Nathan's place, a shop called Old 99 that was a skate gear boutique with a warehouse apartment in the back. This guy had so many drum kits it was unbelievable.

The reason we were dropping the merch off was because we were headed back to Canada and according to a note Mark had given me we needed to be there by the evening to do a radio interview which we were looking forward to. So I phoned John from FRATRICIDE in Vancouver to find out the time and he told me that the radio show was nearly over and Mark had been given the wrong time. We then spent the day record shopping and I found 'Senseless Offerings' while Graham found 'War On 45' and 'This Side Up'. Later we hit an overpriced bar and played pool before getting some cheap swill at a gas station and crashing out relatively early as in the morning we had to drive to the border again.

killsadie

AT THE AMERICAN LEGION HALL

manner farm

IN MANKATO

Baxter

LIVE IN MINNESOTA

brand new unit

brand new unit

brand new unit

JINX, GARY AND BEN IN DENVER

brand new unit

JINX IN DENVER

FOLLOWING THE B.N.U. VAN INTO DENVER

FALLING SICKNESS

LIVE IN PROVO, UTAH

PINHEAD CIRCUS

AT THE WRAPSODY, PROVO, UTAH

YOUTH BRIGADE

MARK STERN IN PROVO, UTAH

YOUTH BRIGADE

AT THE RAVEN IN DENVER

YOUTH BRIGADE

FORT COLLINS WITH TREV ON BASS

THE HAND PAINTED FLYER FOR THE FORT COLLINS GIG

HAIRY IN BILLINGS, MONTANA

OTIS IN THE FRIDGE

OTIS ON THE DRUMS

WILL AT SHRINE HALL

YOUTH BRIGADE

WHAT PRICE HAPPINESS: BILLINGS

FOUR LETTER WORD

JON IN MISSOULA

PINHEAD CIRCUS

DRUNK TREV & CHRIS IN MISSOULA

YOUTH BRIGADE

DRUNKEN TREVOR IN MISSOULA

CHAPTER 70: VANCOUVER COMPLICATION

We arrived back at the Canadian border late in the morning of Friday the 31st of July and approached the guards with caution and baited breath not knowing what would happen, and they just looked at our passports and waved us on. We drove off in disbelief checking the rear view mirror again and proceeded to drive to Gastown between downtown and Japantown in Vancouver to 'The Brickyard' at 315 Carrall Street where we were met with the worst sight imaginable, even worse than Market Street in San Francisco.

The corner where the venue was happened to be the hip Vancouver hangout for every junkie, crackhead, pimp, pusher and walking corpse in the city and we were met by what appeared to be the zombie apocalypse with bums passed out on the floor and various tables while various sex acts went on down the alley next to the club. It turned out that the alley a few blocks over was called Blood Alley, why couldn't they have conducted their sordid business there?

We freaked out a little and drove around the block a couple of times to assess the situation and worked out a plan. We were going to approach the human toilet at a slow speed and park for a moment while I nipped into the bar to find out the load-in time. This seemed like a good plan until in his uncertainty Graham didn't stop and parked slap bang in the middle of the human zoo again. In the stress and heat of the moment we exchanged unpleasantries before I went in and found out the load-in time and we left, the van in silence. We'd been living in each other's pockets for over a month and nerves were starting to fray.

We drove out of the city and bought some food at a supermarket in West Vancouver before eventually heading back to the venue. PINHEAD CIRCUS were there and had been sat outside for an hour witnessing a man overdose on a car in front of them and apparently die. Sex workers were still doing business in the alley while junkies hassled them for money, so after the fastest load-in in history we stayed inside and drank beer. Eric from FRATRICIDE and STRAIN popped in to invite us to stay that night and then went on his way.

The doors opened, the club filled and SUPERCHIEF were up first, their guitarist being Ben from BRAND NEW UNIT's brother Adam. They sounded like 80s West Coast punk and did a cover of D.I.'s 'Falling Out'. We played straight after and went down well to a couple of mohawed slammers. I'd done my usual intro saying we were from the U.K. and after our set one of the Canadian mohawk guys came up and told me it was really cool that we were from the Yukon. Accents eh?

After our set I popped outside the venue to cool off and to see if the street scene was any better and surprisingly by night it was pretty quiet, helped mainly by unmarked police cars speeding by and skidding to a halt every five minutes seeing dozens of people scattering from the shadows ramming their gear into their socks. I returned inside and PINHEAD CIRCUS and YOUTH BRIGADE went down well before we packed up, got hassled by drunks, phoned Eric and went to his girlfriend Hollis' house to sleep.

FOUR LETTER WORD

BYO RECORDS • Post Office Box 67A64 • Los Angeles, Ca 90067 • www.byorecords.com

BRICK WALL PUNK PROMO PHOTO L-R: WELLY, HAIRY, WILL, JON

CHAPTER 71: MY RENTED GUITAR GENTLY WEEPS

It was Saturday the 1st of August and we got up late to an astoundingly healthy breakfast laid on by our gracious hosts Eric and Hollis before trying to organise a phone interview from another note I'd been given, but there was no answer. Eric then took Scooter, Chuck the Pinhead merch guy, Graham and myself to a few record stores while the others amused themselves on a Playstation. I found the NO ALTERNATIVE 'Backtracks' 7" on Subterranean and a BLACK HUMOR bootleg 7".

We returned to the house and then all headed off to an all-you-can-eat buffet at a veggie Indian restaurant then, with filled to capacity stomachs, we headed to the gig. On the way we were waved off the wrong turning by John the promoter and ex-FRATRICIDE vocalist and got lost for a good half hour before finally stumbling back in the right direction to the 'Seylynn Community Recreation Centre Hall' at 625 Mountain Highway in North Vancouver. We loaded in early and bought some beer from a local store and then watched PINHEAD CIRCUS skate while the other bands loaded their gear into the large sports hall in the distance.

PLAN ORANGE, SUPERCHIEF and YAPHET KOTTO played in the echoing hall followed by FOUR LETTER WORD and PINHEAD CIRCUS. There were only 27 people in attendance and according to the promoter the reason being that there was an international firework competition 'The Festival of Lights' going on as well as the BEASTIE BOYS playing downtown. Absolutely nothing to do with absolutely no BEASTIE BOYS or fireworks fans hearing of any of our bands.

We met some appreciative kids at the gig though and then Jon gently wept as he handed his rented guitar back to Ben's brother Adam from SUPERCHIEF to take back to his music store, leaving Jon with Shawn's old one again that was only held together by the stubborn understains. We packed up and drove back to Hollis' place and crashed out.

CHAPTER 72: KILLER WHALES OFF THE PORT SIDE

We woke very early on Sunday the 2nd of August and drove to
see the Stern family fresh from their family wedding the
night before in Vancouver. We met them along with John of
FRATRICIDE and headed off to the Tsawwassen ferry terminal
in Delta, British Columbia. The Sterns were pretty hungover
as YOUTH BRIGADE, PINHEAD CIRCUS and FOUR LETTER WORD all
boarded the ferry to Victoria Island.

We were told that killer whales were sometimes but rarely
spotted in the bay so we spent a good hour staring at
the sea in anticipation to no avail. Deflated we headed
inside and queued up for some veggie burgers and suddenly
an announcement came over the tannoy, "Killer Whales off
the port side". We all ran back outside to catch various
glimpses of them flipping and swimming past following the
ferry, mouths agape like a group of school kids on a trip.

We had everyone else's gear in our van to save money on
the ferry tickets and arranged to meet YOUTH BRIGADE and
PINHEAD CIRCUS onshore on the island and cram everyone into
the mini-bus. But the driving route off had no other exits
and we found ourselves on the Patricia Bay Highway with
no way back. Not knowing what to do we drove the thirty
minutes to Victoria with John FRATRICIDE and located the
club 'The Limit' at 1318 Broad Street. Outside the closed
club a woman from a tattoo shop who'd been told to look out
for some Limeys told us to head to a pub called Steamers,
but right then the two other bands walked up as they'd
managed to bribe a school bus driver to run them into town.

Victoria was known as little England with it's double
decker buses and red telephone boxes, and while being a
bit surreal it almost felt like home apart from the fact
that the sun was out, so we took advantage of the warm
afternoon with a few ales before heading off to our huge
complimentary suite for 15 people and relaxed for a while
before heading back to the Limit for a soundcheck.

We did an awkward soundcheck on the professional stage, the
fire door at the back of the venue open to let the afternoon
sun stream in, and after the soundcheck I went for a walk
on my own and bought some Haida art cards at a gift shop.
Hairy asked why I'd gone off on my own inferring I was
pissed off about something and I explained that I thought
it was important to occasionally spend some time out of
each other's faces. Then the former Bristol, but now local
punk Knowlsey, who I'd met on the CHAOS U.K. tour four
years prior, turned up and we all went for another drink.

We were due to play at 10pm and a few minutes before the
set Hairy announced that he couldn't find his wallet which
contained all his money, bank cards, ID and passport. He
was relatively drunk by this point and completely freaking
out, so we all looked for it while he ran off to phone
home and cancel his bank cards in a panic. While he was
gone I spotted his wallet high on a stage speaker that he
must've left it on during his half-drunk soundcheck and on
his return I declared I'd found it and handed it over, but
instead of thanks he seemed to think I'd been hiding it
all along. Even trying to help was now taken the wrong way.

We were first on and played well in spite of Hairy spending
the entire set standing in front of me straddling the stage
barrier in order to rock pose and as a result he didn't
notice a punk kid reach up and detune his bass mid-song.
I tried to tell him but he was hammered and oblivious. At
the end of the set he threw himself on the floor and rolled
around and I jokingly mocked a kick to his head with no
contact thinking I was just joining in with his wacky punk
rock stage antics, but instead the set ended with him
freaking out and threatening me with violence. I laughed it
off as he couldn't be serious in the state that he was in.

After the set we headed to the large band room at the
back and sat down and everyone was there, YOUTH BRIGADE,
PINHEAD CIRCUS and various friends and family. We all sat
down, the door flew open and in stormed Hairy yelling at

me, "You're just a bully, outside now". I couldn't believe this was happening and it seemed like he was intentionally trying to make a scene, "Calm down, you're drunk". "No I'm not, you're a big bully". He replied like a ten year old. I remained in my seat, "Hairy, I'm not coming outside and I'm not fighting you, go to the van and sleep it off". He gave up and stormed out, probably telling half the packed venue on the way out that he'd been assaulted. Everyone in the room was watching, it was excruciating.

I missed PINHEAD CIRCUS due to all of this unnecessary bullshit and while I was watching YOUTH BRIGADE and talking to Knowlsey a couple of his mates came over and told me that they really liked our band. I looked up to see these tall biker looking guys and they introduced themselves as the DAYGLO ABORTIONS. The DAYGLO fucking ABORTIONS liked our stupid band? This news cheered me up no end and all the unnecessary bullshit evaporated for a moment.

By the end of the night everyone was even more wasted so I sat in the van trying to avoid any more drama, there were crazies everywhere, paranoid drunken accusations, and sometimes you just get sick of partying every night. Soon enough we were waiting to leave and Hairy had to be told to get in the van in order for us to get back to the hotel, which he eventually managed to do falling into his seat, immediately opening the side window and puking all down the side of the white mini-bus sobbing, before passing out.

When we arrived back at the hotel room Scooter from PINHEAD CIRCUS was already unconscious as it was his birthday the following day and he hadn't been able to contain himself so was already hammered the night before. The Sterns reckoned he was so drunk that he smelt like he'd shit himself so they drew all over him with Sharpies while Hairy spent the night in the van alone. I was under no illusions that there was no way we'd ever have been signed to a label like this if it hadn't been for the 90s punk rock goldrush, and I felt for what B.Y.O. had got themselves into at this point.

CHAPTER 73: DUDE, YOU'VE GOTTA HELP ME FIND MY TAPE!

The Sterns left early on Monday August the 3rd and we followed soon after to the ferry terminal in Swartz Bay where we caught the noon ferry back to the mainland. 90 minutes later we dropped John FRATRICIDE off and drove up through Richmond, Burnaby, North and then West Vancouver, before following the Sea To Sky Highway, passing Horsehoe Bay north through British Columbia.

We were treated to the most incredible views along the Sea To Sky Highway with the many islands, inlets and Sounds of British Columbia passing us on the left and the Coast Douglas fir covered mountains to our right. As we were admiring the view we rolled the windows down to take in the sunny afternoon air and I felt something hit my arm. A few minutes later I looked down and saw what appeared to be a dying hornet on the inside of the door so when we stopped for a collective call of nature I removed it.

We travelled north until the Bays and Sounds ended, passing Squamish, Daisy Lake, Whistler Mountain, and then finally we reached Whistler after about four hours, a ski and snowboard resort that looked like it had all been built in one fell swoop in 1992. We stopped with PINHEAD CIRCUS to ask for directions to the venue and I climbed back in the van, shut the door and rested my arm back on the open side window and yeow, the hornet's sting had been left on the van door and was hanging out of my arm which burned with intense pain for a lot longer than seemed necessary.

With rough directions we found the 'Maxx Fish' at 4232 Village Stroll in Whistler and it seemed like a nice club. We were given a free meal and some beer before the set which we pulled off OK considering there was a bad P.A. sound and the crowd didn't want to know, so I made some sarcastic comments but no-one understood or took any notice. After the previous night it felt like the band only had three members and a bassist, who as usual cut the set short.

After we got off stage Mark complained about our short sets but it was nothing to do with three of us. He was also stressing out about the plush Holiday Inn rooms that had been booked for us by the promoter. Obviously expensive and posher than any house I'd ever been in they included full kitchens with brand new washing machines and tumble dryers. Mark was thinking that the money the promoter had put up for these rooms would've been better used in our empty pockets and he was right. We watched PINHEAD CIRCUS before we all sneaked off to the hotel to get some sleep and shower due to our early departure in the morning for the long drive back down the Sea To Sky Highway.

Everyone arrived back to the hotel after the gig in dribs and drabs except for Scooter. A woman at the gig had apparently given him magic mushrooms as it was his birthday and he'd been unable to explain to the hotel clerk which room he'd been booked in, promptly got kicked out of the hotel and went to their van instead. He then couldn't figure out how to get back out of the van and spent all night trying to find his Walkman. Hours later in the middle of the night Trevor went down to check where he was and on opening the van door Scooter grabbed him by the collars with wild staring eyes, "Dude, you've gotta help me find my tape!"

CHAPTER 74: THERE'S A RIOT DOWN AT THE POLICE STATION

It was still getting light as we fell into the van at 7.30am on Tuesday August the 4th with immeasurable hangovers. We left Whistler and drove down the Sea To Sky Highway past the bays and inlets of British Columbia, drinking coffee and gazing at the natural beauty in the silence of the sunlit early morning minibus. We drove to and through Vancouver and onwards to the border by about 1pm and sat nervously for an hour watching sniffer dogs rummage through old ladies' cars, and when it was finally our turn the border guard didn't even bother to look at all our passports.

We pulled into the first petrol station we saw and who should be there but PINHEAD CIRCUS so we changed what was left of our Canadian dollars into U.S. currency at a nearby bank and drove all day to Eugene, Oregon, arriving by about 7pm. We met up with our old pal Mark from Bend at the W.O.W. Hall at 291 West 8th Avenue not long after seeing a car mangled on the freeway fresh from a crash. This was another club I'd been to before four years earlier in this cop town and Mark told us that there'd been rioting recently, one after a SWINGIN' UTTERS gig. PINHEAD CIRCUS arrived just after us and Mark the promoter got a call saying the Sterns who'd been the last to leave Whistler, had been stuck behind a car smash on mountain roads for four hours and wouldn't be arriving until about 10pm.

We drank beer outside and girls hung around Will trying to get in for free. A band played, then we played and during our set YOUTH BRIGADE arrived. The crowd were disinterested so I abused them but as usual they were oblivious. We watched PINHEAD CIRCUS from the bar downstairs on a TV before YOUTH BRIGADE ran through their hits. Outside afterwards we watched a kid apparently on P.C.P. pull a signpost out of the ground while another pulled up on a bike in a ski mask, "Hey man, there's a riot down at the police station". There were apparently also undercover punk cops in attendance so we left and slept at Mark's girlfriend's apartment.

CHAPTER 75: A CLOSE SHAVE WITH A SPEAKER STACK

We ate some breakfast at a café where Mark's girlfriend worked on Wednesday the 5th of August and she gave us discount for the free album we gave her for letting us stay. In retrospect she probably didn't want the free album. It took us about three hours to get back to Bend through the mountains of Oregon with Mark hitching a lift with us, and we ended up back at the Lava Lanes bowling alley car park where I set about cleaning out the van before spending an hour on the phone trying to confirm our flights back home and getting nowhere.

PINHEAD CIRCUS were in the car park too and I asked what band was playing on their van stereo as it sounded good. They told me it was the first album by a band called DILLINGER FOUR. Impressed, I tried to get them to loan us the tape but they were having none of it.

Finally in the early evening we drove to the woods outside Bend to the 'Aspen Hall' at 18920 North West Shevlin Park Road, a community hall next to a big pond. Ponds mean mosquitoes so we sprayed ourselves and drank yet more beer as a precautionary measure. Then LAST MAN STANDING played their straight edge hardcore with a butchering of a MINOR THREAT song and the large crowd seemed up for it.

We played next and the place went bananas with people flying everywhere and monitors all over the place. Stage divers, slamming, circle pit, the whole nine yards. This was one of the best responses we'd had and Jon got into it bouncing all over the stage grinning, Will looked like he was dying in agony in the heat, I did my usual sarcastic malarkey and even Hairy somehow managed a drama free performance.

PINHEAD CIRCUS and YOUTH BRIGADE received the same response but during the YOUTH BRIGADE set a few of us were on the side of the erected stage watching this macho guy next to us throw bottled water out to his friends and conducting with his hands, telling them what to do, how to dance, when to stage dive and when to start a circle pit. It all seemed a bit odd like the hardcore Boy Scouts were in attendance trying to earn their stagediving badge.

We looked on as one of his clever pals climbed the speaker stack and dove off, kicking backwards, and in doing so he toppled the entire stack over. A huge cab scraped down my arm as it fell and landed on a poor kid's head who was sat on the floor next to us with his girlfriend. We helped slowly remove the cab and his head was bleeding but somehow he stayed conscious. A close shave with a speaker stack later we kept an eye on him but he seemed to be okay.

Bands over we helped Mark clean up so he could keep the venue and we swept up and filled garbage bags with all the plastic bottles and cans, then we packed up our own gear and left bidding a final farewell to Mark who we'd got to know quite well throughout the tour.

Next up was the long slog back to San Francisco overnight so we stopped for some petrol before hitting the road and the Sterns were seemingly in a bad mood driving off leaving us and PINHEAD CIRCUS, so we headed south in convoy until 5am, finally giving up and pulling up at yet another motel somewhere just before dawn.

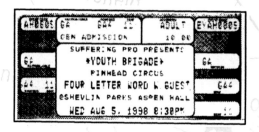

CHAPTER 76: REJECTS FROM SPANDAU BALLET

We checked out late and drove all day on Thursday the 6th
of August and passed from Oregon back into California. We
pulled into a gas station near the State line to fill up
and use the bathroom when completely out of the blue Hairy
blurted out an unrepeatable comment for no apparent reason
and the van fell silent for the rest of the journey.

Van still in silence we drove into Berkeley about 7pm and
PINHEAD CIRCUS needed to buy strings from a music store
before taking us to Telegraph Avenue and Amoeba Records, but
instead I spent half an hour red in the face trying to find
somewhere with a restroom that didn't charge for its use.
We then ate some Greek food so Graham could eat something
vegan before realising that it was getting late, so we
drove into San Francisco quickly and found our favourite
dump Stinky's, the strip joint toilet we'd played before.

We pulled up outside the 'Covered Wagon Saloon' at 917 Folsom
Street at about 9pm as dusk descended, thinking everything
would be fine as this place ran into the early hours, but
no one had mentioned to us that Mark had wanted us there by
7pm because their other brother and bassist Adam was flying
in to join them for the rest of the tour and he wanted to
soundcheck so they could practice before the doors opened.

As we pulled up Mark was stood on the pavement shaking his
head and I just smiled back thinking, "What's wrong now?"
Then as I climbed out he let rip shouting in my face about
how we were late and they needed the backline. I pointed
out that we were merely following PINHEAD CIRCUS and our
arrival time was out of our hands but that didn't seem to
matter. He ranted on mentioning something about us being
constantly late in Canada when we'd been following BRAND
NEW UNIT and how we drank too much. OK, you got us on that
one. After this I was no longer in the mood for another gig
at this sleazy dive so I spent most of the evening in the
van only entering the club to play.

The nice guys that were RETOX turned up to see us and brought us some cider, or hard cider as the Americans call it as normally their cider is just apple juice. Then it was our turn and of course the Frisco retro new wavers didn't like it and one of this crowd of hipsters who all looked like rejects from SPANDAU BALLET heckled us after we finished our song 'Chemical Sunrise' with, "Diarrhoea Rock!" Then someone spat on me so I returned the compliment.

Thankfully for once after six songs we bailed and I flipped them off placing my microphone on the vocal monitor so as to cause screaming feedback. Jon did the same with his guitar and we left these wannabe 80s turds amid a cacophonous feedback din rubbing their spandex arses together in a strange tribal dance to DURAN DURAN and CULTURE CLUB 7"s.

While still trying to push my way out of the packed strip dump to the screech of feedback, Mark appeared and gave me even more grief because we'd already eaten thinking no-one would've bothered making the bands food in this salubrious establishment, but of course they had and again I was on the bosses' shit list. It felt like we were the British whipping boys at this point and I recalled how we'd been told at the start of the tour about how when some of the UK82 punk bands originally toured the States they'd apparently acted like rock stars when they played Southern California. At this point it felt like our nationality meant our cards had been marked before we'd even arrived and any perceived misstep only served to confirm the bias.

My head was completely shot by the time I managed to actually get beyond the bustling throng and I sat outside in the van simmering. The other members of our band gradually joined me and PINHEAD CIRCUS hung around our van with Dave from THE PARASITES in tow. Eventually the freakshow ended after the other bands finished and we waited to leave. We politely declined offers of parties in favour of skipping town and instead drove south until 4am and found another cheap motel somewhere, morale at an all time low.

We checked out of the hotel and into the humid heat of Southern California on Friday the 7th of August and I tried to phone PINHEAD CIRCUS who were staying at Dave from THE PARASITES' house but the number had been disconnected. So we hit the road alone and drove all day on Highway 101 south through California past King City, San Louis Obispo, hitting the coast at Pismo Beach and then the coast road past El Capitán State Beach towards Santa Barbara.

We reached Goleta just west of Santa Barbara and located 'Sniffy's' at 430 South Fairview at the ridiculously early time of 4pm. The place was a large deserted empty store front so we explored the locale and found a health food shop and all bought cheap cold veggie pizza slices while Graham found some baked tofu. As we were sat outside eating on the kerb one of the young store workers burst out of the door, "Are you guys FOUR LETTER WORD?" We replied in the affirmative. "You're playing tonight right? I heard you on the radio, you guys rock!" Tonight was already looking up.

After we'd finished eating like stray dogs on the pavement we moved on to more important matters by grabbing a couple of beers and heading back to the venue at around 6pm. The promoter was now there as well as 7SECONDS who we greeted. Loads of free beer turned up as well as label mates PEZZ from Memphis and we introduced ourselves. PINHEAD CIRCUS soon rolled up followed by YOUTH BRIGADE and we played it cool after the San Francisco incident the previous day.

Rory, Nick and Kris from the label arrived bringing with them Mark's wife Sandi and their house mate Anthony. We hung around and the drinking continued for a while and then PEZZ played first and sounded great. The place was filling up when it came our turn and we tried our best with a good stage sound but it was all to no avail as Hairy was by now bordering on being pass out drunk and almost incapable of playing his instrument.

In the middle of the set he started to undress and took off his shoes, and sick of his behaviour I picked up one of his trainers and threw it into the audience. We finished the set and he had another explosive tantrum in front of just about everyone we knew. He wasn't aware that Graham had been in the crowd and had immediately retrieved his shoe so we strung him along letting him think he had only one shoe for the rest of the night later giving it back to him laughing, but as usual he didn't see the funny side.

PINHEAD CIRCUS did their thing to the usual good response and then it was time for 7SECONDS to take the stage. All fired up and as energetic as in 1984 they rocked the house like no band we'd seen on the tour. All the hits were bashed out and after spending the entire evening down the front playing air drums to all the bands, Steve Youth ran around in between songs banging his head with his hands like he was out of his mind with energy. The stage was invaded and dived from by the crowd and they finished with '99 Red Balloons' and 'Young Til I Die', leaving us slack-jawed in awe. After this YOUTH BRIGADE headlined, to 7SECONDS insistence, and blasted through their Sound and Fury.

Afterwards people were milling about and I talked with Adam Stern and Steve Youth for a while before Chris and Trevor from PINHEAD CIRCUS somehow got everyone together for a B.Y.O. photo session with everyone lined up against a wall inside the venue; 7SECONDS, YOUTH BRIGADE, PINHEAD CIRCUS, PEZZ, all the people who worked at the label and for some reason some clowns known as FOUR LETTER WORD.

It was getting late so we packed up and left with Rory driving us the 90 minutes south east to Reseda and the B.Y.O. staff punk house where all the guys who worked at the label lived; Rory (CHANCES ARE), Nick Mendoza (THE MISSING 23RD), Ron Avila (FINAL CONFLICT and ANTIOCH ARROW) and their friends Maccers, Anthony and Nathan. As thanks for their hospitality we stank their nice house out with our feet and kept everyone awake with our snoring.

CHAPTER 78: WHO WANTS TO PLAY BASS?

We woke up in the hottest part of L.A. in the San Fernando Valley on Saturday the 8th of August and for once we didn't do anything all day apart from eat and try to stay cool. Graham went with Ron Avila to see him practice with FINAL CONFLICT but for once the rest of us needed a break from loud blaring punk rock music. Graham later brought back a few copies of two recent FINAL CONFLICT 7"s courtesy of vocalist Ron Martinez and passed them around.

In the early evening we drove the 90 minutes out to Riverside and 'The Barn' at 1500 West Campus Drive on the University Campus. As its name suggests it was a big venue/barn with a big capacity. We were early and nothing seemed to happen for hours so we just hung around bored until the sound guy finally turned up and we did our soundcheck.

The place filled quite quickly as we were about to start at 8pm and we'd been given some drink tickets five minutes before we were due to go on so we located some weak American fizzy brown water and downed it. We plugged in and played and Rory wanted to do his guest bass slot on our songs 'Chemical Sunrise' and 'Sleight of Hand', but Hairy's fragile ego couldn't take it so Rory just played 'Chemical Sunrise' and reluctantly handed the bass back.

The crowd turned out to be a load of stuck-up types who'd only come for the headlining bands, leaving us with the job of entertaining them when they just wanted us to leave. They found it hard to even raise applause so I made some of my usual sarcastic remarks introducing 'All American War' which as usual went down like the proverbial lead balloon.

We got our set over with as soon as possible, then PINHEAD CIRCUS played to a similar response so I made a point of clapping and cheering loudly in between songs. This didn't impress one young man who saw fit to push me across the dance floor in a mock slam dance to try to shut me up.

After they'd finished we all hung around by the t-shirt
stall outside in the courtyard near the bar and had a
good laugh singing altered lyrics to YOUTH BRIGADE songs
while they played. We were joined by Mark's wife Sandi and
her young nephew Chris Murphy whose father was originally
from Cardiff in Wales. We got along well and I gave him my
number. A year or so later when he visited his grandparents
in Cardiff he phoned me and I showed him around. We have
remained friends since.

Obviously YOUTH BRIGADE went down well to the Southern
Californian crowd, then 7SECONDS pulled off an even more
astounding set than the previous night with Kevin Seconds
jumping into the crowd across the stage barrier to sing
with the kids. I positioned myself on the short flight of
stairs at the side of the stage taking photos but even I
wasn't safe and he made his way over to shove the microphone
in my face to join in with 'If The Kids Are United'.

Bands over the crowd cleared ultra fast in the usual
American style as the club played some muzak to empty the
place, and we packed up our gear and merch before piling
into the van with the B.Y.O. workers and headed back to the
B.Y.O. punk house back in Reseda to sleep.

CHAPTER 79: GOODBYE AMERICA, FUCK YOU AMERICA!

We came around on Sunday the 9th of August, drank coffee and
sat around until around lunchtime and then we all headed
over to Mark Stern's house for a barbecue by the pool.
We arrived and everyone was there; the Sterns, 7SECONDS,
PINHEAD CIRCUS, a few friends of the Sterns, and for some
reason FOUR LETTER WORD were allowed in.

Scooter, Trevor, Chris and Otis a.k.a. PINHEAD CIRCUS took
it upon themselves to start a belly-flop competition off
the diving board while a few people swam and we sat in
the shade on the other side of the pool opposite everyone
else. Sandi, Mark and Shawn cooked the food and we all had
a solid refuelling before driving over to West Hollywood
and Beverly Hills and the 'Troubadour' at 9081 North Santa
Monica Boulevard for the last gig of the tour.

The Troubadour seemed like one of those clubs where the
employees acted more like rock stars than the rock stars as
we loaded in the gear. Chris, Trevor and I went to buy some
beer at a liquor store across the street and on our return
I was told that I'd missed the soundcheck and Scooter had
filled in on vocals, so I sat in the PINHEAD CIRCUS van for
a while drinking and laughing with them until I was notified
that we were on in five minutes. I said I'd be right in
after I'd downed the pint bottle and Trev and Chris didn't
believe me. The next thing I knew I was on stage trying to
look energetic with a gut full of suds weighing me down.

We didn't sound too bad as the stage sound was good and Rory
got up to play bass on 'Chemical Sunrise' again while I
finished the tour with, "Goodbye America, fuck you America"
to the large crowd of large skinhead types and young punk
kids. At the start of the set I'd pointed out that it
was our last gig thanking all the bands, and afterwards
everyone thought we'd split up. The last set of the tour
left a bittersweet taste like a weight was lifted, but also
left a hollow feeling knowing that was it all over.

Jon and I headed outside to cool off after we'd finished playing and who should walk up and introduce himself to us shy Limeys but Kevin Seconds and we had a lengthy chat with him about all sorts of stuff before Shaun from DAMNATION walked up and we exchanged pleasantries as we hadn't seen him since the gig at Public Storage in Anaheim at the start of the tour. We loosely arranged to meet him for an interview later but it never came to pass.

PINHEAD CIRCUS played their kick arse punk rock for the last time with us dedicating their song 'Clear A Path' to us as we were heading home. Dennis from SOCIETY GONE MADD who I'd drawn some artwork for a few years previous came up and introduced himself and then YOUTH BRIGADE began.

As you'd expect the place went off for these local hardcore legends, and a violent circle pit of huge skinheads swirled until halfway through the set when one skinhead managed to dodge the vigilant security and climbed on stage throwing a Nazi salute before diving back in with a grin on his face. We looked on from the balcony and as soon as he hit the crowd, the security and about twenty guys beat him across the packed dancefloor and we watched as what looked like a small circle pit moved across the crowd and out the door. All we could see was a storm of punks and skins pounding an unseen object.

Shawn started ranting on stage about Nazis and how his family were Jewish and had escaped the holocaust and the crowd were on his side and reacted accordingly. We were told later that supposedly these huge anti-Nazi street fighters in the audience were from a Latino gang, whoever they were they dealt swift and uncompromising justice.

By the end of the set we were all stood on the side of the stage stood next to 7SECONDS jumping up and down to YOUTH BRIGADE and pushing each other on to sing into the microphone looking back at each other and laughing like kids. The main problem with this legendary Hollywood club was the over-zealous security, who took it upon themselves to police the joint to the point where even the bands had trouble getting on stage. If any punks decided to climb the boards they were thrown down the side stage ramp by these ultra macho goons, some straight out of the back door.

7SECONDS came on to a rapturous response, kicked into their hits and the place went insane. Throughout the whole three gigs they'd been playing all the old stuff from 'The Crew' and 'Walk Together, Rock Together', as well as a few newer numbers and some covers. They flew through all the classics like 'Regress No Way' and 'We're Gonna Fight' and the crowd was building into a frenzy.

After watching so many people get thrown off stage by the burly bouncers, Nick from the label, myself and a few others already on the ramp at stage right concocted a plan by shouting into each other's ears during the last song. Then on the last chorus of 'Walk Together, Rock Together' we all simultaneously ran on, grabbed the nearest microphone and sang along. This incited the crowd to follow suit, the stage was invaded and it completely overwhelmed the security in one huge singalong chorus for a grand punk rock finale to the tour.

After the gig we talked with the Sterns and 7SECONDS in the parking lot at the back of the club for a while before bidding them farewell and climbing into the van. Then I quickly grabbed my camera and jumped back out preserving the moment on film for posterity and we drove away.

There had been an idea floating around that we were going to somewhere called Magic Mountain the next day to ride roller coasters. I'd never ridden one and never wanted to so I planted the seeds of dissent and within fifteen minutes there were two groups; Chris, Trevor and Otis from PINHEAD CIRCUS as well as the B.Y.O. crew were all heading to Wally World while the FOUR LETTER WORD gang as well as Scooter and Chuck from PINHEAD CIRCUS were going record shopping.

We reluctantly accepted an invitation to stay one last time at Shawn Stern Concentration Camp due to its proximity to record shops, bought some food at a supermarket and headed back. We ate and I fell asleep but I was soon awoken by a raised voice, "What are you guys doooing? Why is there a bag of food on my freshly polished floor? You're a bunch of pigs!" I closed my eyes and pretended to be asleep.

B.Y.O. ALBUM AND TOUR PROMO SHEET WITH EMBRYONIC DATES

CHAPTER 80: THE VINYL SOLUTION ON BEACH BLVD

We got up and got out of Shawn's on Monday the 10th of August before we did anything else wrong, and I split the last of the tour cash between the five of us, including Graham who I counted in as a band member and we each got about $100. Will and Jon grabbed their cut and followed Hairy to the Third Street Promenade in Santa Monica, Hairy left them to buy some more gigantic trousers, Jon spent all his on a trinket for his girlfriend and Will went bargain hunting and picked up a belt for a mere $30, discovered it was the size of a watch strap and had to take it back.

Graham, Scooter, Chuck and myself on the other hand spent the whole day driving the length and breadth of L.A. We first drove to Huntington Beach and Vinyl Solution on Beach Blvd, a fairly priced goldmine where I picked up some long wanted rarities in the form of the first FEAR LP, the first VANDALS 12" as well as that DILLINGER FOUR LP I'd heard blaring from the PINHEAD CIRCUS van in Bend, Oregon.

Next we drove to Greene Records, where Ron Martinez of FINAL CONFLICT worked and Graham picked up the first WARZONE 7" when after much umming and aahing I reminded him he'd probably never see it again. Finally by early evening we headed all the way out to Alto Loma and Doctor Strange Records who were such nice people that they kept the place open for us, gave us cans of pop, free shirts and free CDs. Even more vinyl gems bagged, we headed all the way back to Venice Beach to pick up the others from Shawn's before driving all the way back to Reseda to sleep.

While the others were losing their enthusiasm on Tuesday August the 11th, Graham, Hairy and I drove over to Hollywood for more record shopping and we discovered some interesting places. Record shopping concluded, we headed over to the B.Y.O. office on Glencoe Avenue one last time and I spent the last of my cash at the Vans outlet around the corner on shoes for my better half and son back home.

B.Y.O. closed for the evening and we drove out to Reseda where we met up with everyone and then drove straight back to Hollywood where FOUR LETTER WORD, PINHEAD CIRCUS and Kris the B.Y.O. office under manager visited the Old Spaghetti Factory on Sunset Boulevard for our last night. While there we ate spaghetti then headed off to a pool hall to shoot pool and booze it up and we ended up drunk on the balcony until around 2am when we drove back to the punk house in Reseda for one last night.

ARTCORE ISSUE #13 WITH ORIGINAL TOUR REPORT

CHAPTER 81: TERMINAL DEPARTURES

Time was of the essence on Wednesday the 12th of August as we had to get to the airport by 12:45pm just after noon, so we said some difficult goodbyes to PINHEAD CIRCUS and the B.Y.O. kids, some of the nicest people we'd ever met. We didn't realise we'd never see them again. Then we drove over to B.Y.O. and rammed some goodies into our jam-packed bags, the B.Y.O. guys took a couple of snaps of us, we all hugged and then Nick ran us over to LAX spot on time.

The airport was packed, hours flew by checking in and before we knew it we were on the plane leaving America, homeward bound and it was over. The ten hour flight was its usual pinnacle of boredom, the highlights being some aeroplane food and a couple of microscopic beers. I passed out, woke up, watched the sun go down, then watched it come back up and it became Thursday August the 13th. I had a polite conversation with a guy sat next to me from Birmingham while the green fields of the U.K. came into view. It was a crisp, bright morning as we circled London in a holding pattern and soon enough we landed, flashed our passports, waited what seemed like an age for our luggage and walked through customs.

Our reliable friend Mark was supposed to be meeting us in a borrowed van from the community centre we rehearsed at, but he was late so I called home to hear that the van had broken down. I hung up the phone, turned around and somehow he was there with the van fixed so we threw our bags in, threw ourselves in and drove to Wales. We dropped Graham off in Bristol and got back to Cardiff at midday where my better half Tina had laid on a veggie barbecue and I saw my young son again after seven weeks. Jon went straight to his girlfriend's house, Hairy hung around for a while then disappeared and Will left with his mother and brother. A few familiar faces appeared and disappeared throughout the afternoon and I was so tired and completely spaced out that it was starting to feel like I'd dreamt the entire thing.

CHAPTER 82: GHOSTS ON THE HIGHWAY

Sooner or later the road always came to an abrupt end and you had to go home, back to quiet rooms where the floor stood still beneath your feet even though it still felt like you were moving, time stretching out before you with nothing left to listen to but the ringing in your ears and the ticking of the workplace clock. All the noise just suddenly stopped and you were left to reflect on all that had passed with a vague sense that something was missing.

The summer 1998 tour had lasted 55 days, taken around 13,000 road miles and 11,000 air miles, spanning 36 gigs over 13 U.S. States and 4 Canadian provinces with 3 cancellations. Jon, Will and myself only saw each other twice throughout the rest of August and September and at some point Hairy was told he was out of the band. We saw him again a year or so later when he appeared in a pub we were in, sat down and apologised for his behaviour on the tour saying that on reflection he'd only been out for himself. We never saw him again. The following year in 1999 a 'cease and desist' order from a law firm for a major label boy band who'd trade marked our name illegally ended our contract with B.Y.O. seeing our next and best album binned upon release. On the upside 1999 meant we also now had a daughter, Heidi, so it was just as well more tours like this didn't come along.

As a result of the lawsuit and a big negative statement from the label, Jon and Will drifted in and out of the band, Will at some point drifted out permanently and we eventually lost touch. I kept the band going in one form or another for another decade or so with various members, touring the U.K. numerous times and the East Coast of the U.S. in 2007 and Jon and I still write music to this day.

Eventually the Stern Brothers' Punk Rock Bowling idea grew to the point where it was a huge international punk festival that took precedence over B.Y.O. and eventually they vacated the site in Marina Del Rey and it was later redeveloped into apartments, this legendary punk rock label nothing more than a memory and some unsold stock.

By pure coincidence exactly twenty years later, I ended up moving to Arizona where we'd started our tour by nearly starting a small riot and a place I never thought I'd visit again. Life is a bit like going on tour though, you start out with all these ideas of what it might actually be like but you never really know where it's going to take you until you get there, the journey being the destination.

Sometimes it can seem like none of it is real even when it's happening, sitting with friends in the baking sun in a parking lot waiting for a club to open, watching ants weave their way through the cracks in the broken earth. Looking back we were a bit like those ants, tiny punk bands moving slowly along the cracks on the map all but invisible to the larger world above, each oncoming obstacle seeming insurmountable at the time but somehow we always made it over that next mound of dirt and onwards to the horizon never to return, like ghosts on the highway.

We sometimes rush through our lives as if we aren't really experiencing them, so it's good to pause for a moment every now and then to look into these cracks and let the bustle race on by above. I'd do it all again in a heartbeat of course although realistically it's never going to happen, a bit like how I told myself I'd keep in touch with all those people I met along the way, but time and distance put paid to that. After all, it's not just the lives that the band touches, it's the lives that touch the band, so let this book stand as a tribute to those transient friendships, half as long but twice as bright.

Even though these tours were like volunteering to be sort of homeless and nomadic for months at a time, for some reason I still wonder if one day I'll get that call and find myself again among friends gazing upwards at the desert night sky, staring out of the van window for countless hours taking in sweeping panoramic views or jumping out of the van at a gas station somewhere in a strange town at dusk, with nothing more to go on than an address on a scrap of paper, for more directions to the outskirts of town.

SKATING IN NORTH VAN LOAD-IN BEHIND: SCOOTER (L), TREV (R) & CHRIS

Yaphet Kotto

SEYLYNN HALL, NORTH VANCOUVER

ERIC FRATRICIDE, HOLLIS, CHUCK, THREE PINHEADS AND TWO F.L.W.

SHAWN, JON, WILL, TREV, CHRIS, MARK, SCOOTER, WELLY, CHUCK, OTIS, JAMIE STERN

ON THE B.C. FERRY TO VANCOUVER ISLAND

THE SEA TO SKY HIGHWAY, BRITISH COLUMBIA

CHUCK PIEKARSKI MANS THE MERCH IN VICTORIA, B.C.

LEAVING CANADA: THE BORDER PEACE ARCH, SURREY, B.C./BLAINE, WA

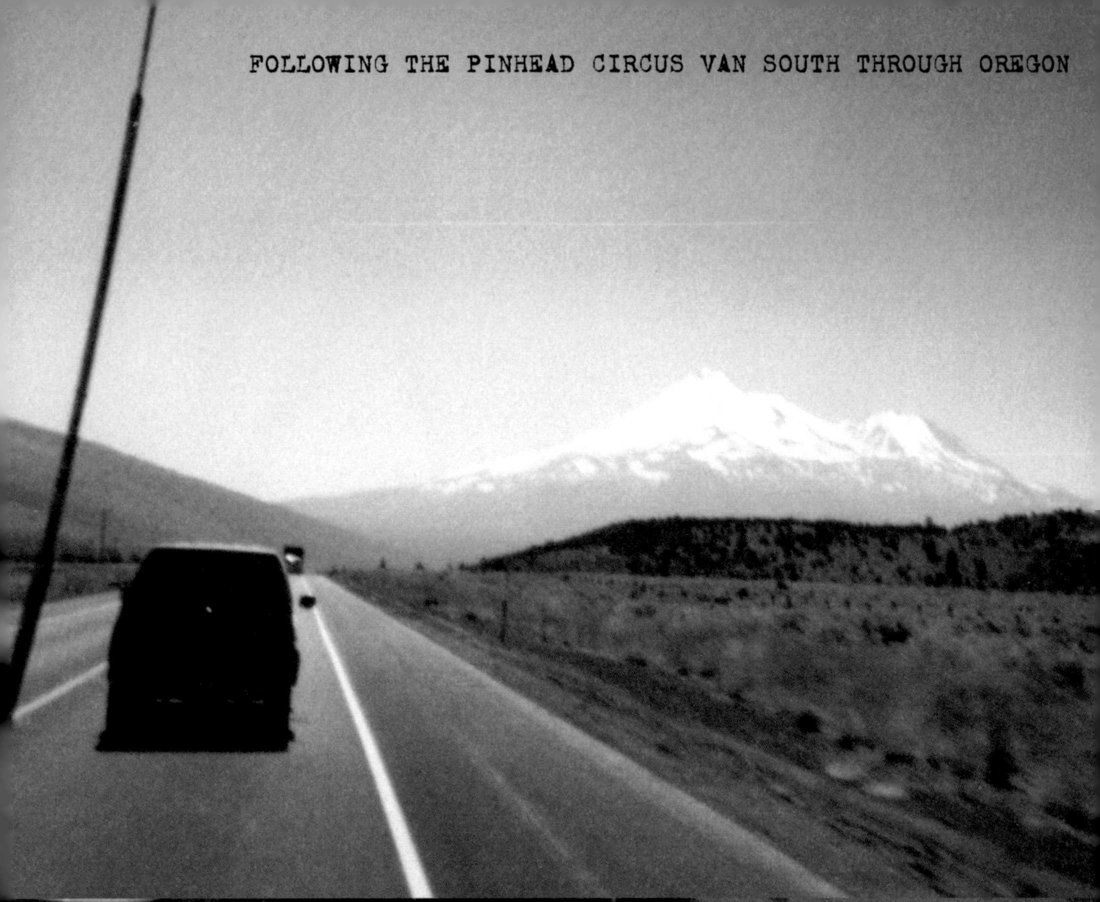

PINHEAD
CIRCUS

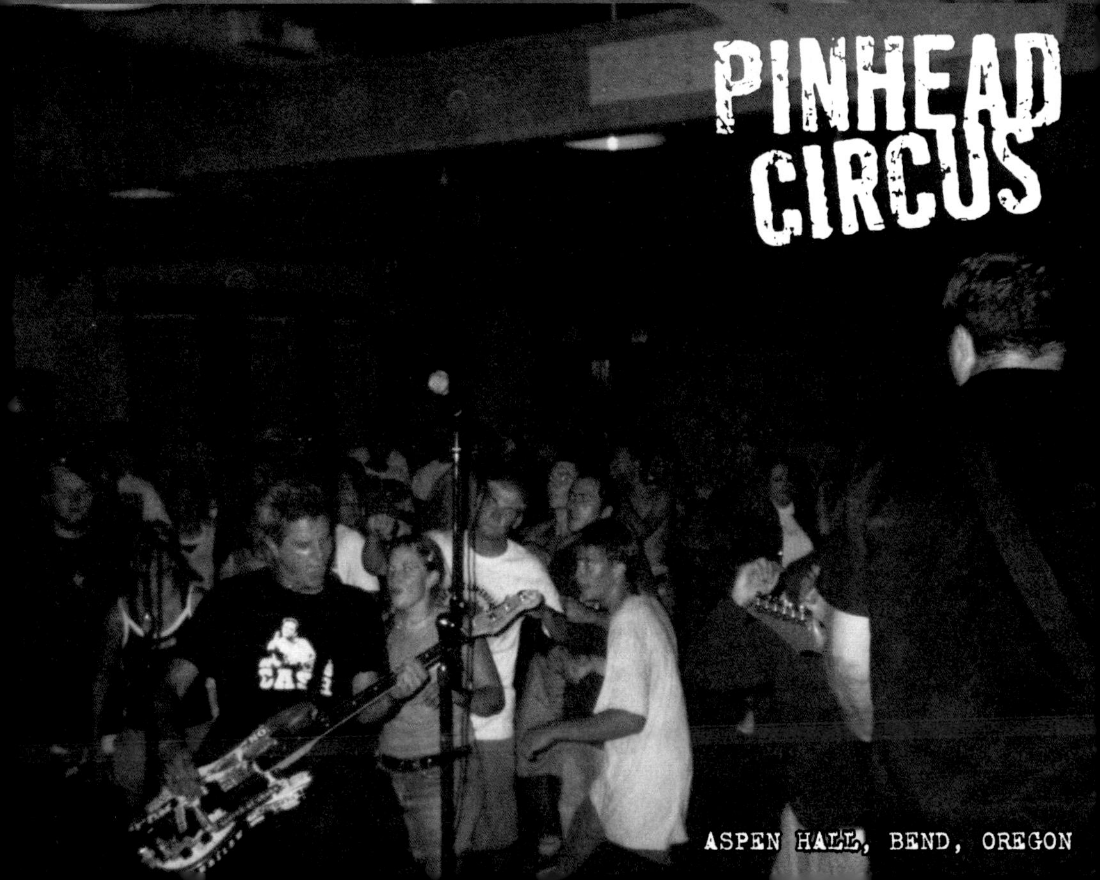

ASPEN HALL, BEND, OREGON

YOUTH BRIGADE

MODEST PROPOSAL IN BEND

FOUR LETTER WORD

STINKIN' UP GOLETA

PEZZ

THE EYES HAVE IT: SNIFFY'S

PEZZ

ONE LAST LOOK IN GOLETA

7SECONDS

I STILL BELIEVE IN GOLETA

7 SECONDS

WALK TOGETHER, ROCK TOGETHER AT SNIFFY'S

7 SECONDS

WALK TOGETHER AT THE BARN

7SECONDS

LIVE AT THE BARN, RIVERSIDE

FOUR LETTER WORD

RORY ON THE BASS

FOURLETTERWORD

JON IN HOLLYWOOD

PINHEAD CIRCUS

AT THE TROUBADOUR

HAPPY HOUR AT THE TROUBADOUR

YOUTH BRIGADE

YOUTH BRIGADE

SINK WITH CALIFORNIA IN L.A.

7 SECONDS

COLOURBLIND IN HOLLYWOOD

BUT AFTER THE GIG: SHAWN, KEVIN SECONDS & MARK

A NASTY PIECE OF WORK TOUR DATES 1998

Thursday 25th June - Phoenix, AZ - Vortex

Friday 26th June - Los Angeles, CA - Bollocks

Saturday 27th June - Los Angeles, CA - Whisky a Go Go

Sunday 28th June - Anaheim, CA - Public Storage

Monday 29th June - Stockton, CA - Chavas

Tuesday 30th June - San Jose, CA - The Usual

Thursday 2nd July - San Francisco, CA - Stinkys

Friday 3rd July - Berkeley, CA - La Val's Pizza

Sunday 4th July - Lake Tahoe, CA - Rojos

Monday 5th July - Mckinleyville, CA - Six Rivers Brewery

Tuesday 6th July - Eureka, CA - The Vista

Thursday 9th July - Bend, OR - Evil Sister Saloon

Friday 10th July - Surrey, BC, Canada - Bridgeview

Saturday 11th July - Kelowna, BC, Canada - The Pit

Sunday 12th July - Calgary, AB, Canada - The Republik

Monday 13th July - Edmonton, AB, Canada - Rebar

Tuesday 14th July - Saskatoon, SK, Canada - Louis Pub

Thursday 16th July - Winnipeg, MB, Canada - West End

Friday 17th July - Mankato, MN - American Legion Hall

Thursday 23rd July - Provo, UT - Wrapsody

Friday 24th July - Denver, CO - The Raven

Saturday 25th July - Fort Collins, CO - Starlight

Sunday 26th July - Billings, MT - Shrine Hall

Monday 27th July - Great Falls, MT - The Center

Tuesday 28th July - Missoula, MT - Jays Upstairs

Wednesday 29th July - Seattle, WA - RKCNDY

Friday 31st July - Vancouver, BC, Canada - The Brickyard

Saturday 1st August - Vancouver, BC, Canada - Seylynn Hall

Sunday 2nd August - Victoria, BC, Canada - The Limit

Monday 3rd August - Whistler, BC, Canada - Maxx Fish

Tuesday 4th August - Eugene, OR - W.O.W. Hall

Wednesday 5th August - Bend, OR - Aspen Hall

Thursday 6th August - San Francisco, CA - Stinkys

Friday 7th August - Goleta, CA - Sniffy's

Saturday 8th August - Riverside, CA - The Barn

Sunday 9th August - Los Angeles, CA - Troubadour

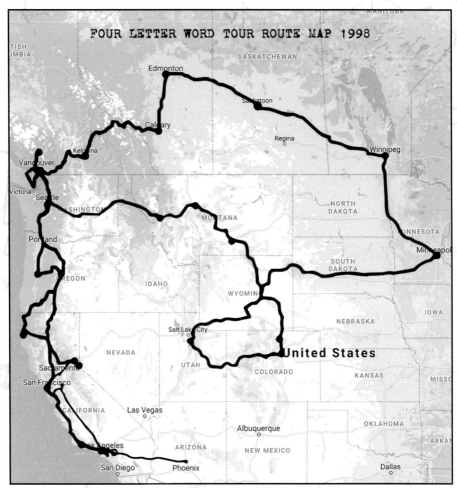

FOUR LETTER WORD TOUR ROUTE MAP 1998

38 U.S. STATES VISITED ON BOTH TOURS IN BLACK
(PLUS FOUR CANADIAN PROVINCES: BC/AB/SK/MB)

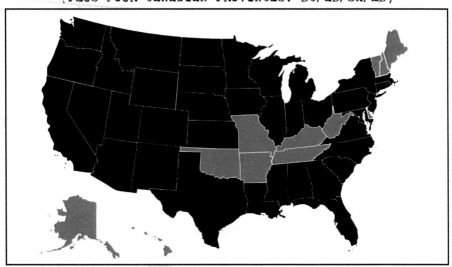

THANKS

Tina, Kieran and Heidi. Jon, Will, Hairy and Graham. Chaos,
Gabba, Victor, Marvin, Pat and CHAOS U.K. Shawn, Mark, Adam
and YOUTH BRIGADE. David Gamage and Earth Island. Kip-Xool,
Mike, Jimmy, Brian, Marc, Joey (RIP) and EYEHATEGOD. Kevin,
Bobby, Steve, Troy and 7SECONDS. Johnny, Max, Darius,
Spike, Kevin, Greg and SWINGIN' UTTERS. Scooter, Trevor,
Chris, Otis, Chuck and PINHEAD CIRCUS. Gary, Jinx, Ben,
Gabe and BRAND NEW UNIT. Marvin, Ceylon and PEZZ. Jon, Jon,
Jeff, Gary, Bob and TURMOIL. Chris, Dave and JOHN COUGAR
CONCENTRATION CAMP. Rory, Kris, Nick, Ron and the B.Y.O.
Crew. Maccers, Anthony and Nathan of the Reseda punk House.
Jamie Stern, Sandi Stern, Becca Porter, Chris Murphy and
family. Monica and the Topping family. Skinny, Scott, Rob
Phelps, Greg MAGGOT, Jim Martin, Al Quint, Jimmy PUBLIC
NUISANCE, Roy NAUSEA, Ralphy DISASSOCIATE, Val JESUS CHRUST,
Kev and Rat VARUKERS. The Stringer family. Chris Barrows,
Bob Suren, Josh and CHAPTER ZERO and Jeff in San Clemente,
Shawn BRAIN BOMB, Oliver Withöft (RIP) and Century Media,
Cesar and DOGMA MUNDISTA, TOXIC NARCOTIC, Red Skull, Pig
Nose and ASSRASH, Sid, Jon and MISERY, Rob, Karl and IMPULSE
MANSLAUGHTER, PIETASTERS and INSATIABLE. Maximum Rock 'n'
Roll, Katz Flipside (RIP), BEELZE BULLIES, John and Kris
and RETOX, Vinnie and Charlie in Fort Collins, and you.

THEY MADE ME SUPPLY A MUGSHOT

ABOUT THE AUTHOR

Originally from Cardiff in Wales, Welly's lifelong obsession
with punk rock began in the late '70s where he soon found
himself designing his own home made record covers. As a
result, after high school he studied graphic design at
print school and art college for four years and has been
a graphic designer for punk bands and labels for over 30
years since with over 170 published releases to date.

While still in high school, after finding out what a fanzine
was from the pages of Maximum Rock'n'Roll he began creating
his own Artcore, in late 1985, printing a few dozen copies
of the first issue on the high school photocopier in January
1986. He continues to publish Artcore to this day with 40
issues and 16 vinyl fanzines released to date.

After writing lyrics from an early age he co-founded FOUR
LETTER WORD in 1991 taking up the role of vocalist and
after one 7" EP in 1995 they signed to YOUTH BRIGADE's Los
Angeles based B.Y.O. Records in 1997 for the story you just
read. They released a total of four albums and eight EPs
and singles before calling it a day 20 years after forming.

After FOUR LETTER WORD Welly formed the short lived STATE
FUNERAL on vocals before being asked to join VIOLENT ARREST
for their last two releases followed by the one-off studio
project SIGNAL CRIMES with three members of HERESY. With
30 years of bands and 20 releases under his belt he now
thinks it's time for the kids to have their say.

He also ran two D.I.Y. punk rock record shops/stalls,
Damaged Records (2004-2008) and the aptly named Ghost Town
Records (2012-2014) in Cardiff, Wales, and was involved in
promoting and making flyers for gigs and all-day charity
benefits in Cardiff and Newport from the 1980s onwards.

After the tours he visited the U.S. numerous times with his
family before relocating to Arizona in 2018.

GRINDCORE STENCHFEST!
SUNDAY JULY 10
4PM
FROM ENGLAND
CHAOS U.K.
DISASSOCIATE
AND
MAGGOT
PUBLIC NUSANCE
NEW REPUBLIC
TURMOIL
AT
WETLANDS
161 HUDSON ST.
...WHY ARE THERE SO MANY FLIES IN HERE?

CHAOS U.K.
-TURMOIL-
-EDISON-
-LOST CAUSE-
BABY HEAD
JULY 12TH

CHAOS U.K.
WITH SPECIAL GUESTS
WED. JULY 13
AT THE
PHOENIX TAVERN
$5.00

FACTORY
737 W. BROAD
TORNADO PRESENTS: All Ages • 8pm UPSTAIRS
CHAOS U.K.
From England
ONE HUNDRED PERCENT
TWO FINGERS
IN THE AIR
PUNK ROCK

ENGLAND'S PUNK LEGENDS
CHAOS U.K.
AND
EYEHATEGOD
SCROG
Tuesday
$5
9PM
July 19
PUNK
The Nlone Lounge
all ages

ALCOHOLIC SLUTS PRESENT
CHAOS U.K.
with
EYEHATEGOD
FREE FRIDAY JULY 22nd BEER
RC BRIDGE LOUNGE
1201 MAGAZINE
PH. (504) 523-9190

Monday July 25
CHAOS UK
EYEHATEGOD
ETHYL
MERMAN
RIOT SQUAD
ALL AGES
ONE HUNDRED PERCENT
TWO FINGERS
IN THE AIR
PUNK ROCK
DOORS
9P.M.
$5
PRESENTED BY
k29
TWISTED KI
GALAXY CLUB Deep Ellum

SHOWCASE THEATRE
PRESENTS
ALL AGES
NOW OPEN
WEDNESDAY AUG. 3
CHAOS U.K.
PLUS SPECIAL GUESTS
IN THE AIR

FRIDAY AUGUST 5
CHAOS U.K.
EYE HATE GOD
ACME INC.
SLIP
$6
CACTUS CLUB
18 AND OVER WELCOME

RENO 94
CHAOS U.K.
It's A SWINDLE Man's!
EYEHATEGOD
Toxic NARCOTIC
UNISCENE
NoiseGATE
GAUGE
MONDAY AUGUST 8TH
$6 ALL AGES 7PM
FALLOUT SHELTER RENO 702-324-3188 for info
PUNK FEST

CHAOS U.K.
SWINGIN' UDDERS
MISERY
ASS RASH
AUGUST 19th 8PM
ALL AGES FIVE BONES

FROM ENGLAND
CHAOS UK
NEW RED ARCHIVE RECORDS FROM SAN FRANCISCO, CA.
THE SWINGIN' UTTERS
AND PUNKS FROM SOUTHERN, CA.
THE MAGGOTS
THU. AUG 25
18 & OVER 10 PM
DOORS AT 9 $6
GROG SHOP
1765 COVENTRY CLEVE. HTS
321-5588
THREE CHORDS AND FUCK YOU

DIRECTIONS TO THE OUTSKIRTS OF TOWN

WELLY ARTCORE ★

COLORADO

GRAPHIC DESIGN/LAYOUT/PHOTOS/ILLUSTRATION: WELLY

(SOME 1998 PHOTOS BY GRAHAM SLEIGHTHOLME OR WHOEVER WAS HOLDING THE CAMERA)

ARTCORE

★ 2021